D0036764

CONTENTS

Introduction 5

And, the Twenty-Seventh Letter
    of the Alphabet 7

OMG WTF IQ 9

OMG, Prime Minister 12

Major Fraud 14

Bat Bomb 18

Beating the Bomb 21

Beating the Odds 23

Turning Yellow Into Gold 26

Sable's Stable 29

The Money Pit 31

The Halifax Tragedy 33

Wash Out 36

Everyone's Tea Time 39

Deep in the Heart of Wartime 42

The Sentence of One Hand
    Clapping 44

The Man with the Golden Arm 46

De Grote Donorshow 49

Donor 150 51

Pain in the Red 54

Red Light, Green Light 57

Fandemonium 59

Fans and Peanuts 61

Killing Charlotte Braun 63

Lunch and a Murder 66

The Passion of the Money-Laundering
    Extortionist 69

Stolen Smile 71

Unvandalism 74

Dissolving Medals 77

A City Fit for a King 79

Cola Enforcement Agency 81

Mr. Acid 83

High and Outside 85

Performance Enhancing Injuries 88

Wood Medalist 91

Out of Sync 94

To Kill a Sparrow 97

The Cobra Effect 99
The Aptly Named Snake Island 101
Where the Bodies Go 104
Slaying the Silver Ball 107
The Free City of Tri-Insula 110
The North in the South 113
Where the Bags Go 116
Finding the *Titanic* 119
The Two Soviets Who
    Saved the World 122
Blame Cuba 125
Invading Canada 128
The Pig War 130
Bacon of the Sea 133
McLibel 135
McHotDogs 138
Potato Parties 140
Fire Horse Women 142
Pumpkin Saving Time 145
Trick of Treats 147
One-Armed Bandits 150
The *Zong* 153
The Overwater Railroad 155
Rats! 158
The Assault of Amagansett 160
War Games 163
Missile Mail 165
Space Mail 168
Star-Spangled Moon Banners 171
Marooned on the Moon 174
D-Day's Doomed Dry Run 177
If Day 181
Unhip to Be Square 184

Limonana 186
A Date with Destiny 188
Super Seed Bank 190
Thou Shalt Not Die 192
Norwegian Wood 194
A Festivus for the Peruvians 196
Ice Cream, You Scream 198
Put on a Happy Face 200
The Perfect Crime Scene 202
The Usual Suspects 204
Pruning Up 207
Temporary Blindness 209
The Bird is the Word 211
A Princely Meal Fit For a Pauper 213
The Greatest Thing Since 1928 216
Color by Number 218
Orange Goes Green 220
Gone Bananas 222
Radioactive Red 224
Bull's Eyes 226
Blood Falls 228
Leaving Marks 230
No Man's Land 233
Garbage City 235
The Trash Collectors 237
Pork Project 239
The Great Syrup Caper 241
Oil Baron 244
Onion Ring 246
Lift Off 249
Skyscraper Caper 251
To Infinity and Beyond 254

INTRODUCTION

Truth is stranger than fiction. Someone once said that. I have no idea who, but he or she is right—the most astonishing things around us aren't made up; they're real. Mark Twain once allegedly observed why: "Fiction is obliged to stick to possibilities; Truth isn't."

For more than three years, I've been writing about these interesting facts and the fascinating stories behind them. For example, everyone knows that airlines occasionally lose luggage, but what happens when they find it months later? If it never goes back to its owner, where does it go? We know that people landed on the moon. But what would have happened if they couldn't get home? And what happens to the stuff they left behind, like the American flags?

In this book, you'll find the answers to those questions, and the stories behind 100 of the world's most mind-blowing pieces of trivia. Each entry includes a fact, the story behind that fact, and a related bonus fact. I've tried to connect them all in some way, piggybacking off one another, but they don't form a logical line. You'll zigzag from McDonald's (why can't you get a hot dog there?) to Daylight Saving Time (and pumpkins . . . you'll see!) pretty quickly. We'll look at the strangest reality TV show in history (it's Dutch) and somehow wander to the world's strangest traffic signals (they're North Korean), all in the span of about ten pages. Together, we'll jump around from one thing to another, always finding something interesting along the way. Chances are, wherever you wind up, it'll be someplace interesting. (For more of this sort of thing, go to my website, *www.NowIKnow.com*. There you'll find a lot more random facts and the stories behind them—did you know Abraham Lincoln created the Secret Service . . . on the day he was fatally shot?)

As each story proves that truth is stranger than fiction, you'll be able to declare *now I know*—and that's half the battle. So welcome to the world of the utterly strange, which couldn't be made up because it couldn't be true, except that, as we all know, it is. Somehow.

AND, THE TWENTY-SEVENTH LETTER OF THE ALPHABET
WHY THE "AND" SYMBOL IS CALLED AN AMPERSAND

The English alphabet contains twenty-six letters, with two of the letters—"A" and "I"—themselves also constituting words. However, another character—the ampersand (&)—was also, at times, included in the alphabet. And amazingly, the word "ampersand" is probably a by-product of the symbol's inclusion.

The ampersand was developed along with the rest of the alphabet back in the early years of Rome in the seventh century B.C.E. Romans would occasionally combine the letters "E" and "T" into a similar symbol, representing the word "et" meaning "and." It was included in the Old English alphabet, which was still in use into medieval times. When Old English was discarded in favor of the modern English we are familiar with, the ampersand maintained its status of "member of the alphabet" (to coin a phrase) to a degree, with some regions and dialects opting to include it until the mid-1800s.

Except that it was not yet called an ampersand. The & sign was, rather, referred to simply as "and"—which made reciting the alphabet awkward. As Dictionary.com states, it was (and is) odd to say "X Y Z and." So, people didn't. Instead, our lexicon developed another saying: "X, Y, and Z, and by itself, 'and'"—but instead of saying "by itself," the Latin phrase *per se* came into favor. The result? "And *per se*, and," or, muttered quickly by a disinterested student, "ampersand."

Why the inclusion of the ampersand in the alphabet fell out of use is anyone's guess, but there is a good chance that credit goes to the ABC song we are almost all familiar with—that is, the one that shares its tune with "Twinkle, Twinkle, Little Star" (and borrows from Mozart's "Ah Vous Dirai-je, Maman"). That song was copyrighted in 1835, around the time that the ampersand started falling out of favor with the rest of the ABCs.

BONUS FACT

Although Old English included the ampersand, it did not include a few letters we use today, notably "J," "U," and "W." "J" and "U" did not become letters until the sixteenth century (they were, instead, represented by "I" and "V," respectively), and "W" became a letter independent of "U" soon after.

OMG WTF IQ
THE CENSORING OF A SUPER-COMPUTER

If you're a *Jeopardy!* fan, and particularly one who watched the show in 2004, there's a nearly 50 percent chance you've seen Ken Jennings on the screen. That year, Jennings, a software engineer from Utah, won seventy-four consecutive episodes spanning 182 calendar days (due to weekends, the show's week off in the summer, and interruptions from various tournament and special episodes). His total prize money from his seventy-four wins and one second-place finish exceeded $2.5 million.

Jennings earned another $800,000 from subsequent *Jeopardy!* appearances to date. In 2005, he returned for the *Jeopardy! Ultimate Tournament of Champions*, involving 145 of the game's biggest winners over the previous two decades. Jennings came in second, earning $500,000. And in February 2011, he and the champion of the *Ultimate Tournament*, Brad Rutter, faced off against Watson, a computer built by engineers at IBM.

Watson beat the two human champions, earning $1 million for a pair of charities. Jennings earned $300,000 and Rutter $200,000 for third place. (Each of the humans donated half their winnings to charity as well.) Watson's programming team fed the computer more than 200 million pages of data from sources such as Wikipedia, news articles, dictionaries, and thesauruses. Although Watson succeeded in beating Jennings and Rutter, its creators realized that it had a flaw—Watson had a difficult time, to say the least, understanding slang and the nuances of the English language. Around the same time the *Jeopardy!* episode aired, Team Watson introduced a new data source to the machine's databanks—entries from the slang and shorthand website Urban Dictionary.

Founded in 1999, Urban Dictionary invites users to suggest and vote on words and phrases that have entered our collective lexicon but aren't generally accepted, at least not by sources such as *Merriam-Webster*'s or the OED. Over the years, the website has gained acceptance in more formal environments; for example, according to www.thesmokinggun.com, it was used as a source by federal prosecutors when a suspect posted to Facebook about how he intended to "murk" someone. ("Murk," per Urban Dictionary, means, "to physically beat someone so severely, he ends up dying from his injuries.") But it also includes a bunch of terms that contain vulgarity and, when used without an appreciation for the connotation of the terms, shouldn't be used in certain environments.

Watson lacked that appreciation. As reported by *Fortune*, the computerized *Jeopardy!* champ "couldn't distinguish between polite language and profanity," even using some choice, bovine-related language when telling its programmer-researchers that they were incorrect about something. The researchers added profanity filtering to Watson's programming, but this proved inadequate given the extensiveness of Urban Dictionary.

Finding no alternative—unless one wants to build a genius robot that swears like a sailor—the researchers removed Urban Dictionary from Watson's database.

BONUS FACT

Ken Jennings's incredible *Jeopardy!* run almost got derailed before it truly started. On his first episode of the show, the Final Jeopardy! question (or, in *Jeopardy!* parlance, "answer") was "She's the first female track and field athlete to win medals in five different events at a single Olympics." Jennings, with $20,000 going into Final Jeopardy!, led his two opponents. In second place was Julia Lazarus, who had $18,600. Lazarus waged $3,799, but got the answer incorrect, writing "Who is Gail?" (she later told host Alex Trebek that she had no idea what the correct answer was), bringing her total to $14,801. Jennings wagered $17,201; if he got the answer right, he'd win, but a wrong answer would send him home (and in last place for the day). He wrote "Who is Jones?"—a somewhat ambiguous response. Trebek immediately stated that the judges "will accept that; in terms of female athletes, there aren't that many." (The right Jones? Marion.)

OMG, PRIME MINISTER
WHERE OMG COMES FROM

OMG, as anyone under the age of twenty-one (and practically everyone else, at this point) knows, stands for "oh my god!" The acronym is commonly used in text messaging but it predates the era of ubiquitous cell phones. In fact, it predates the era of ubiquitous phones—cellular or otherwise.

The *Oxford English Dictionary* has long been the standard-bearer of what belongs in the English language and what does not. Unlike other dictionaries, which stay faithful to a long-established vocabulary of words, the OED tries to adapt to the lexicon of the day. So when words and similar terms enter our collective parlance, the OED's editors may end up adding them to their dictionary. In March 2011, "OMG" was one of the added terms, along with "muffin top" ("a protuberance of flesh above the waistband of a tight pair of trousers") and "LOL," meaning "laugh out loud."

But the OED doesn't simply define the word. It also attempts to track down the term's origins. Sometimes, it fails, of course; take for example the term "rubber game," which is the deciding game in a bridge match or baseball series. The term has been in use for decades, if not centuries, but no one—at least no one the OED can find—knows where it comes from.

OMG, on the other hand, has a known first use. It isn't from the mid-1990s, when the Internet started on its path to ubiquity, or even from the 1980s, when services such as Prodigy and Compuserve dominated the early digital communications space. The term OMG dates back to 1917 and, strangely, involves Winston Churchill, at the time a British Member of Parliament, and, of course, the future Prime Minister of that nation. That year, the recently retired Admiral of the British Navy, John Arbuthnot Fisher, wrote Churchill about rumors of new honorifics potentially coming down from the crown. Specifically, per the OED, he wrote: "I hear that a new order of Knighthood is on the tapis—O.M.G. (Oh! My God!)—Shower it on the Admiralty!"

The OED doesn't mention Churchill's reply, if any, and does not explain why Admiral Fisher needed to both use the acronym and immediately write out its full meaning. The OED does, however, provide the next earliest known use—1994, in an online newsgroup about soap operas. The author asked the rest of the group, simply, "OMG, what did I say?"

BONUS FACT

On June 1, 1943, actor Leslie Howard—best known for his portrayal of Ashley Wilkes in *Gone with the Wind*—died when the Nazi Luftwaffe shot down the civilian airplane he and a dozen others were aboard. (The UK did not consider the route to be part of the war zone; the Germans clearly disagreed.) But the actor's death was, according to one widely believed account, not simple chance. As the theory goes, the Germans targeted the plane because they were led to believe that Winston Churchill, who was in Algiers and hoping to return to Great Britain, was on the plane. He, of course, was not.

MAJOR FRAUD
HOW A DEAD MAN FOUGHT THE NAZIS

During World War II, the British government tightly controlled information about casualties. Providing such details—who died, when, and where—could provide the Nazis and the other Axis powers with information they'd not otherwise have, and risk British and Allied efforts around the globe. At the same time, the government felt obligated to communicate the war's events to its citizenry. These two desires were in obvious tension, and the government found a happy medium by releasing death notices to the newspapers.

Although these death notices came with the risks noted above, they also offered opportunity. On June 4, 1943, the *Times* published the announcements of the death of three officers and that of actor Leslie Howard. One of the officers was a member of the Royal Marines, a Major William Martin, who drowned in late April of that year.

Kind of. Major Martin hadn't actually died. He couldn't have—because he never actually existed.

With the war in full swing at the end of 1942, seizing control of the Mediterranean was high on the Allies' list of military objectives, and the eventual success in North Africa would make that even more likely. But capturing other locations could be an even larger boon. Sicily, for example, served as a key island; as Winston Churchill reportedly commented, "Everyone but a bloody fool would know" that Sicily had to be next on the Allies' punch list.

So the UK decided to try and play Hitler for a bloody fool. The plan, called "Operation Mincemeat," was developed in part from a memo written by future *James Bond* author Ian Fleming. Operation Mincemeat involved leveraging the Nazi intelligence department's cozy relationship with Spain by planting some disinformation on the Spanish shore. The disinformation came in the form of a pair of dossiers outlining, among other things, the Allies' plans to invade Greece, Sardinia, and Corsica, all while feigning an attack on Sicily. To deliver these dossiers into the hands of the Spanish and, ultimately, the Germans, British intelligence's MI5 unit called the fictitious Major Martin into duty. Or, more accurately, they threw a corpse wearing his clothes—and holding the dossiers—into the sea.

In January 1943, a thirty-four-year-old homeless Welsh man named Glyndwr Michael died of liver failure caused, indirectly, by ingesting rat poison. Michael's death was difficult to determine and his parents had already died, making him—his dead body, that is—a solid stand-in for the Royal Marine that British intelligence was about to create. Michael's body was dressed in a manner suitable for Martin's rank and stature, even down to the high-quality underwear. (Quality underwear was rationed at the time and difficult to obtain, but a major in the Royal Marines would certainly be wearing some.)

Intelligence created a backstory for him, including a fiancée named Pam, and gave him love letters, a receipt for an engagement ring from a London establishment (dated April 19, 1943), and a picture of her (really of a clerk in MI5). To finish the ruse, Major Martin was given ticket stubs to a London theater, dated April 24, and—to make him appear careless—an ID card marked "replacement." All these items were placed in a briefcase, along with two copies of the Mediterranean war plans, one for British troops and one to be forwarded to U.S. commanders. The second copy was created simply to justify the use of a briefcase in the operation.

The body was taken aboard a British submarine, which surfaced on April 30. That day, the corpse was tossed into the waters, the briefcase tied around the loop of the fallen major's trench coat. It washed up on shore as planned. The official cause of death by the Spanish medical inspector was "drowning" and, because Martin's belongings suggested that he was a Roman Catholic, the examiner declined to perform an autopsy. The documents, after a few days, made their way into German hands—despite British "efforts" to recover them. On May 13, the Spanish returned the body to the British so that it could properly buried, and it was clear that the briefcase had been opened and its content analyzed.

The Germans bought into Martin's persona, "determining" that he was on a flight from Britain to Gibraltar to deliver the sensitive documents—a belief strengthened by the June 4 death notice in the *Times*. German leadership shuffled their defenses to buttress their positions in Greece, Sardinia, and Corsica, leaving Sicily mostly unguarded. When Allied forces invaded Sicily on July 9, the Nazis thought it was a feint, as the documents suggested; by the time the Germans reinforced the island on July 12, it was too late. Roughly two weeks later, the Axis began their retreat from the island.

BONUS FACT

Famed baseball manager Billy Martin wasn't a William Martin. His real name was Alfred Manuel Martin Jr., but Alfred Sr., his father, skipped town when Billy was very young. Around the same time, Billy's maternal grandmother started calling him "Bello"—the Italian-masculine for "beautiful"—and Billy's mother, Joan, adopted "Billy" as his nickname. Because of Joan's hatred for her ex-husband, she hid Billy's true name from him; according to Wikipedia, it was not until Billy started school that he learned his true name. When the teacher called "Alfred Martin," Billy ignored her, believing that she was referring to someone else.

BAT BOMB
USING BATS IN UNCONVENTIONAL WARFARE

During the final days of World War II, the United States, apparently believing that Japan was unlikely to surrender otherwise, dropped atomic bombs on Hiroshima and Nagasaki. The death toll from these two bombs numbered as high as 250,000 when one factors in those people who died up to four months later due to burns and radiation sickness. Research into the creation of an atomic bomb began in 1939, and the Manhattan Project, which developed the science behind the weapons in earnest, began in June 1942. But in March 1943, the United States was developing another weapon that would have spared many thousands of lives.

Unless, that is, you count the lives of the millions of bats that would have died in the process.

In the mid-1940s, many Japanese buildings were still constructed out of wood and paper, which, of course, were flammable. If the United States Army could figure out a way to start fires in a large number of buildings spread out over a wide area, the Japanese infrastructure and economy would suffer but the direct loss of life would be relatively small. But that seemed impossible. Napalm strikes could start fires everywhere, but they wouldn't spread. Carpet-bombing with many small warheads would increase the area of the strike but most likely wouldn't cause many fires. And of course, the death toll from either of those routes could still be large.

But a few months before the Manhattan Project got underway, a dental surgeon named Lytle Adams came up with the idea to use bats—those nocturnal flying mammals—as part of the strategy. As he would later tell *Air Force Magazine*, after seeing millions of bats flying around caves in Carlsbad Canyon in New Mexico, he immediately thought that they could be used as a way to spread firebombs throughout Japan. He collected a few of them himself, did a little research, and found that even tiny bats weighing well under a pound could carry three times their weight in explosives. He pitched his plan to the military (a procedure that was apparently not uncommon at the time) and the brass agreed that this was something to look into.

Adams's theory was straightforward. Collect a million bats and strap timed incendiary devices to their backs while they hibernate. Stick a thousand of them each into a thousand bombs designed to open at high altitudes. Fly over Japan at night, drop the bombs, and then let the bats fly around. When daybreak comes, the theory went, the bats will hide in dark places—and given where they are, the most common hiding place will be attics. The timer ticks down and shortly after, without obvious explanations, hundreds of thousands of Japanese buildings start to burn to the ground.

The idea soon became more than a theory. By March 1943, the U.S. military had identified a suitable population of bats, having located a series of caves in Texas that were home to millions of the flying critters. For the next year or so, at the expense of $2 million ($25 million in today's dollars), they tested Adams's theory. Except for one major problem—at one point, some bats got loose resulting in a major fire at the base—the military believed that the bat bombs could actually work. One report placed their effectiveness at ten to thirty times more effective (measured by the number of fires they would start) than conventional incendiary devices.

But the final report on the bat bombs issued in mid-1944, though positive, noted that they would not be ready for combat for another year. Due to the slow timetable, the military canceled the project before it could be fully developed.

BONUS FACT

Bats eat insects (among other things), including malaria-carrying mosquitoes. In the 1920s, a researcher named Charles Campbell proposed building "bat towers" that would provide a roost for bats during the day so they could feast on the mosquitoes at night. An active one exists at the University of Florida, but the most famous one is probably the Sugarloaf Key Bat Tower in the Florida Keys. A fish lodge owner named Richard Perky built the Sugarloaf tower in 1928 with much fanfare—and one big problem. According to Atlas Obscura, when Perky put the bats into the tower, they flew off to find some bugs to eat—and never came back.

BEATING THE BOMB
THE MAN WHO SURVIVED HIROSHIMA AND NAGASAKI

Twenty-nine-year-old Tsutomu Yamaguchi was in Hiroshima, Japan, about to return home from a business trip, when he realized that he'd left his *hanko*—a personal seal used for endorsing documents—back at the office. His return trip was interrupted by history. The U.S. bomber *Enola Gay* dropped an atomic bomb on Hiroshima; its center of impact was fewer than two miles from where Yamaguchi's walk took him. Nearly 140,000 people died in the explosion but Yamaguchi survived. The force of the blast knocked him to the ground, permanently destroyed his left eardrum, temporarily blinded him, and caused severe burns across part of his body. Nevertheless, after seeking shelter, he managed to return to his hometown for treatment the next day.

Two days later, Yamaguchi—still bandaged and deaf in his left ear—returned to work. He was recounting the events of the Hiroshima bombing with a supervisor when the images he saw just a few days earlier began to appear before him again. But Yamaguchi was not suffering from a flashback. He worked in Nagasaki, and he was, again, fewer than two miles from the point of impact of an atomic bomb.

And again, he survived. This time, he did so with no new injuries, although the explosion ruined his bandages from the first blast and caused him to run a fever.

Yamaguchi is the only person recognized by the Japanese government to be a double *hibakusha*, the term given to survivors of the atomic bomb drops. *(Hibakushas* are entitled to a specific kind of government support.) Probably, in total, between 100 and 300 people survived both blasts, but only Yamaguchi has thus far earned the distinction.

His health, after the blasts and radiation exposures, was decidedly mixed. He wore bandages for most of his young adult life, lost hearing in his left ear (as noted above), and went bald. His children all believe that they, too, inherited health problems caused by the radiation. However, Yamaguchi was (after a long recovery) able to return to work and live a relatively normal life—and a long one at that. He passed away in January 2013 at age ninety-three.

BONUS FACT

Some call Yamaguchi the world's luckiest person for having survived both bombs. If so, what does that make Kathleen Caronna? During the 1997 Macy's Thanksgiving Day Parade in New York City, a *Cat in the Hat* balloon escaped its handlers, knocking over a lamppost. According to an account in *The New York Times,* the lamppost struck Caronna in the head, sending her into a coma for nearly a month. Nine years later, New York Yankees pitcher Cory Lidle crashed his plane into an apartment building overlooking the East River, killing him and his flight instructor. The plane's engine landed in one of the apartments—owned by Kathleen Caronna. This time, she wasn't harmed, as she wasn't home, but the apartment's bedroom was destroyed by the ensuing fire.

BEATING THE ODDS
HOW MATHEMATICIANS BEAT THE LOTTERY

The running joke is that the lottery is a tax on those who can't do math. But on occasion, we see the opposite—people who are very, very strong in math not only play the lottery but also walk away with their pockets flush with newfound money.

Cash WinFall is a rather generic lottery game in Massachusetts. Pick six numbers out of forty-six. Get them all correct, win the jackpot. There are prizes for getting two numbers right (a free ticket), three ($5), four ($150), and five ($4,000) as well—in total, your odds of winning something are better than 1:7. Drawings are held twice a week (Monday and Thursday) and tickets cost $2 each. The jackpot begins at $500,000, but if no one wins it—and it has only been won once in the game's history—it progressively increases until it hits $2 million, when it is reset.

The state makes more than $10 million each year on the game. And a few times each year, as reported by *The Boston Globe*, a bunch of players also make out like bandits. The details are a bit hazy as those who beat the game are loathe to talk about it. But the basic story is as follows.

When the pot breaks that $2 million ceiling but goes unclaimed, it gets reset to $500,000 for the subsequent drawing. But instead of simply resetting the $2 million jackpot to $500,000 and keeping the $1.5 million (or more) overage, the state rolls the excess money into the secondary prizes. During these "rolldowns," the secondary prizes can, and have, hit ridiculous amounts, depending on the amount of excess money in the pot and the number of tickets purchased for the rolldown drawing.

Take, for example, the payouts as of July 14, 2011. Because of the nearly $1.9 million of excess money available, and because relatively few tickets were sold, all the secondary prizes were greatly increased. Instead of winning $5 for hitting three of six numbers, you would win $26. Instead of winning $150 for hitting four of six numbers, you'd get $802. Instead of winning $4,000 for hitting five of six, you'd cash out to the tune of $19,507. (And historically, that's a low amount for a rolldown; once, the five-out-of-six prize was more than $100,000.)

Say you spend $100,000 on the tickets, each $2. That's 50,000 entries. The odds of getting four of six numbers correct are about 1:800, so you will roughly break even from that alone. You'll hit three or six about 1,000 times—that's $26,000. And you may hit that five of six mini-jackpot once or even twice, adding another $25,000 to $100,000 to your saving account—and yes, that is on top of the $100,000 you have already recouped.

And this is exactly what some people are doing. A statistical rundown suggests that purchasing that same $100,000 all but guarantees breaking even, at worst (unless someone wins the $2 million-plus grand prize, in which case there's no rolldown from which to benefit). One couple, the Selbees—who run a gambling/investment firm out of Western Michigan—spent more than $300,000 on Cash WinFall tickets just before the July 14 drawing. It was not the first time the Selbees tried to exploit the rolldown drawing: To date, they have claimed over $1 million in prizes.

The lottery has taken some measures—for example, limiting the number of tickets a person can purchase at one time—to prevent this loophole from being further abused. (And the press and visibility around the opportunity should take care of it, regardless.)

BONUS FACT

In 1999, a New Yorker named Jesus Leonardo was eking out a living doing odd jobs, painting homes, and cleaning windows. On occasion, he'd try his luck, though—not at the lottery, but on the ponies. He'd go to a New York City OTB—off-track (horse) betting—establishment and place a wager or two. One night, like many before, he threw away his losing tickets. But that night, a correction came over the wire a short time after, turning one of his losers into a $900 winner. Unfortunately, the ticket was in the garbage, and without the ticket, he was unable to cash out his winnings. The OTB manager allowed him to sift through the hundreds of discarded tickets that evening, and although Leonardo did not find his ticket, he found two others worth a total of $2,000. He spent the next ten years doing more of the same, turning ticket sifting into his full-time job. It paid him, on average, about $40,000 to $50,000 a year. (Leonardo has since moved on; New York's OTB shut down at the end of 2010.)

TURNING YELLOW INTO GOLD
HOW TO WIN AT THE TRACK (KIND OF)

In the book *Bringing Down the House*, author Ben Mezrich recounts the story of a group of blackjack players, many from MIT, who systematically took casinos for millions of dollars. The blackjack team's system, which requires solid math skills, is designed more to avoid casinos' rules than to exploit the rules of blackjack itself. If anything, the book best demonstrates how buttoned up the gambling world is when it comes to loopholes, aiming to ensure that you can't beat the house.

But that doesn't stop people from trying—and, on occasion, succeeding.

In the 1970s, Barney Curley was a gambler known well in betting circles around Northern Ireland and throughout the Emerald Isle. Looking for an edge, he concocted a scheme that would not only end up working, but worked so well that Irish bookmakers ended up changing their betting rules. It started when he realized that one particular Irish horse racing venue only had one phone line, and it led to a public pay phone.

Curley raised a horse named Yellow Sam and had its trainer prepare it for a specific race at the track in question, Bellewstown, located about a forty-five-minute drive north of Dublin. The decision to focus the horse on this particular race, combined with the fact that the targeted race typically featured amateur jockeys, meant Yellow Sam would have an excellent chance at winning.

But the real money wasn't in winning the race's prize purse. Curley could make much more by betting on his horse to win, especially if the bookmakers put Yellow Sam as a prohibitive underdog. Curley's plan helped make that happen. Before running at Bellewstown, Yellow Sam raced in a handful of events, all under bad conditions, and fared poorly. The gambit worked. The horse developed a reputation as being slow and not that competitive, and when Yellow Sam was entered in the race at Bellewstown, it started as a 20-to-1 underdog.

Under-handicapping horses, as this error is called, is nothing new, and odds makers have a long-standing system to account for it. As bets come in, the odds makers adjust the handicap to reflect the betting activity; that's why the odds on any given sporting event change over time. Most bookies wouldn't accept very large bets from unknown gamblers or, even worse, from known professionals such as Curley. He needed a way to get a lot of small bets entered without the bets being communicated back to the odds makers at the track—which is why Bellewstown was selected. In the end, that single pay phone was the key to the operation.

Race day was June 26, 1975. Leveraging his network of friends, family, and even hiring some others, Curley distributed his life savings—roughly £15,000 Irish pounds—to his compatriots. He gave each of them between £50 and £300 and a sealed envelope with instructions. Curley sent them to bookmakers' offices in their locales. Ten minutes before the race began, each of the bettors placed wagers on Yellow Sam to win.

Fifteen minutes earlier—unbeknownst to the off-site accomplices —another of Curley's friends faked a family emergency. The friend, Benny O'Hanlon, walked into the phone booth and pretended to call his "dying aunt," offering her solace in her final moments. No one was willing to force O'Hanlon off the phone, thereby precluding the off-site bookmaking offices from reconciling the wagers before them. When the race started, Yellow Sam remained a 20-to-1 underdog, and, of course, won. Curley's £15,000 investment earned him £300,000, or, accounting for inflation and exchange rates, about $2.25 million in early 2013 money.

Because the operation was entirely legal, albeit sneaky, the bookmarkers were obligated to pay Curley his winnings. They did so in £1 notes, filling over 100 bags with cash. And, to prevent others from abusing this loophole in the future, bets of greater than £100 now must be placed at least thirty minutes before the race begins.

BONUS FACT

Voltaire, the French writer and philosopher, was quite wealthy—and garnered his wealth in a manner similar to Curley's. From 1728 to 1730, the French government created a lottery intended as a fundraiser. Voltaire (then in his mid-thirties) and a colleague realized that the government had made a mistake—the prize pool was larger than the amount of francs it would take to purchase all the tickets. So the two set off to buy as many lottery tickets as they could. Voltaire earned roughly 1 million francs in the gambit.

SABLE'S STABLE
AN ISLAND OF TINY HORSES

Travel about 150 miles southeast from Halifax, Nova Scotia, and you'll hit something: Sable Island. You may not see it coming—positioned precariously on the northern Atlantic edge of the North American continental shelf, Sable Island is a small, treeless crescent of sand. At its widest point it runs not quite a mile and is only thirteen square miles in area. No one has been born there since 1920 and, except for a handful of transient researchers, no one lives there, either.

Unless you count the few hundred horses.

Sable Island is home to 350 to 400 short, stocky horses, which over generations have found ways to thrive in the unfriendly terrain they call home. No one owns them—they're feral and roam the island freely.

How did they get there? Although many believe the horses' ancestors were stranded on the island after a shipwreck (Sable Island has a history of causing such disasters), that's not the case. During the French and Indian War, Great Britain deported thousands of French settlers, known as Acadians, from Canada, stripping them of their property in the process. One merchant hired to assist in this forced relocation was a man named Thomas Hancock (uncle of the now-famed American patriot John Hancock). Hancock took some horses owned by the relocated Acadians for himself and, for reasons that remain unclear, relocated them to Sable Island.

Today, this species of horse is called the Sable Island Pony. They are not truly ponies, however; the name is a misnomer, likely given to them because they are smaller than most horses. The vast majority of Sable Island Ponies live on the island. The only other place they're found is at Shubenacadie Wildlife Park in Nova Scotia; the Canadian government moved a few there to ensure the species' preservation. But at this time, that may be unnecessary. The horses' Sable Island habitat is protected by Canadian law, which mandates that the creatures be allowed to live on the island without human interference.

BONUS FACT

The deported Acadians were relocated to many different places—some to other New World colonies, some to England, some to France. A group of those sent back to France later returned to the New World, settling in the then-Spanish colony of Louisiana. There, these Acadians revived their culture, one that still survives today. But we don't call it "Acadian." We call it by a similar sounding word developed over time: "Cajun."

THE MONEY PIT
THE HIDDEN TREASURE (MAYBE) IN NOVA SCOTIA

Buried treasure. The idea that one of us—armed with nothing more than a shovel and an X-marked map—can stumble into unknown riches has romanticized those words. Some buried treasure may be on Nova Scotia's Oak Island, home of the so-called "Money Pit."

Discovered at the tail end of the eighteenth century by a sixteen-year-old, the Money Pit goes down at least ninety feet and contains man-made items at that depth. Exploring further has proven difficult because of cave-ins and flooding, which have resulted in six deaths. (Some ascribe the difficulty to a series of booby traps set by whoever buried the items.) We don't know what's down there, but we do know that there's *something* in the pit, which, by almost all accounts, shouldn't be there.

Like most legends involving buried treasure, though, there's reason to believe that the Money Pit is a myth. One popular theory is that the pit is a naturally occurring sinkhole, which at one point swallowed up some tools and other materials in the area. This would explain the unnatural objects located at extreme depths. While many explorers of the Money Pit may be exercising questionable judgment, at least one well-regarded person probably made his way there. In 1909, Franklin Delano Roosevelt allegedly made an attempt to find treasure buried within (there's a picture of him and some friend at the site during an excavation attempt). FDR—and everyone else since—came up empty-handed.

Those who believe that treasure exists at the unreached bottom of the pit cite a number of stories and theories. Allegedly, at about eighty or ninety feet, lies a large stone with symbols carved into it. Attempts to decipher the message have yielded a promise of riches: "Forty feet below, two million pounds lie buried." But that stone was last seen in 1912, and no images of it exist today. It may have existed; it may be the stuff of legend. If it's true, it's led to incredible theories as to what's buried deep below. Some people believe it to be pirate treasure; others think that Spanish Armada sailors or British troops fleeing after the American Revolution dumped items of value there. Another theory holds that at the close of the Seven Years' War, French troops moved the coins held at the Fortress of Louisbourg (on mainland Nova Scotia) there.

No one is certain what lies in the pit, and the mystery will likely go unsolved for many decades. Currently, Oak Island is privately owned, making further exploration of the Money Pit contingent on the whim of its owners, who have shown little interest in allowing for future, dangerous expeditions.

BONUS FACT

Where's the most likely place to find buried pirate's treasure? Long Island, New York. William Kidd, a Scottish sailor executed for piracy in 1701, is widely believed to have buried some of his loot, with the intention of using it as leverage if he were ever brought to trial: This tactic obviously failed. We know for certain that he buried some treasure on Gardiners Island, a small island off the north coast of Long Island, as the treasure was unearthed and used as evidence against him at his trial.

THE HALIFAX TRAGEDY
THE LARGEST MAN-MADE ACCIDENTAL EXPLOSION

On December 6, 1917, an explosion ravaged Halifax, Nova Scotia, killing 2,000 people and injuring 9,000 others. But this mass disaster was not triggered by natural events. The explosion was, entirely, man-made.

Just before 8:45 A.M. on that day, the SS *Imo*, an empty Norwegian passenger and freight ship, and France's SS *Mont Blanc*, collided. The *Mont Blanc*, a cargo ship, was loaded with munitions aimed at supporting French efforts in World War I. The *Mont Blanc* caught fire, and although its crew safely made it to shore, the language barrier—the crew spoke French, while the native Halifax residents spoke English—probably prevented any warnings from being heeded. Twenty minutes later, before hundreds of onlookers, the *Mont Blanc*'s payload caught fire, and the ship exploded.

The explosion's intensity was roughly one-seventh to one-fifth that of the atomic bomb that struck Hiroshima. The *Mont Blanc* itself was instantly vaporized; a fire plume shot up more than a mile in the air. Roughly one square mile around the blast area was destroyed and rendered uninhabitable; structural damage to buildings was recorded as far away as ten miles from the epicenter of the explosion. An earthquake-like shake was recorded seventy-five miles away, and the explosion could be heard more than 100 miles north and 200 miles west of the blast. The blast was so powerful that a half-ton piece of the ship's anchor mast shot through the skies, landing more than two miles from the blast site. (The fragment is now part of a monument placed roughly near its landing spot.)

The aftereffects were also considerable. The explosion set off a tsunami that struck the waterfront with sixty-foot-high waves. It also caused a black, sooty "rainfall" for ten minutes after the blast, covering survivors in debris. The Canadian military lost one of its key buildings, the Royal Naval College of Canada, destroyed in the explosion.

The catastrophe is widely considered the worst man-made accidental explosion in history, when factoring in not just the size of the blast but also the number of causalities, the radius of the damage, and the loss of property. The death toll was so immense that more Nova Scotians died in the explosion than in World War I.

It might have been worse, too, but for intervention from the south. People from the Boston chapter of the Red Cross and Massachusetts's public safety officials traveled to the scene almost immediately after the disaster. Nova Scotia has been thanking Boston since, selecting an evergreen tree each winter and sending it to the city. In recent years, Boston uses the gift from Halifax on Boston Common as the city's official Christmas tree.

BONUS FACT

As noted earlier, the atomic bomb dropped on Hiroshima was roughly five to seven times as powerful as the blast from the Halifax explosion. We know this in part because, for decades after the Halifax disaster, North American media outlets used the event as a yard-stick for measuring other bombs, underscoring the event's significance. For example, when *Time* magazine reported the bombing of Hiroshima, it explicitly stated that the bomb was seven times stronger than the event that caused carnage in Halifax, three-and-a-half decades prior.

WASH OUT
WHAT HAPPENS WHEN LOTS OF WATER MEETS LOTS OF SALT

Lake Peigneur is located in Louisiana, 125 to 150 miles west of New Orleans. If you'd visited it thirty-five years ago or so, you would have found a freshwater lake that, at its deepest, was only about ten feet, well stocked with lots of fish appropriate for the environment. And if you were there on November 20, 1980, you would have seen a 150-foot-high oil derrick disappear into a lake barely deep enough to sink a sailboat.

Texaco, an American petroleum company (since acquired by Chevron), was drilling in Lake Peigneur, hoping to find oil roughly 1,400 feet (430 meters) below the water's surface. We're not entirely sure what happened that day—when 150-foot structures disappear into ten feet of water, there will always be more questions than answers—but more likely than not, the Texaco engineers made a small mistake. Their 14-inch (.35 meter) drill bit was off the mark and went a bit sideways. Normally, that would not be a big deal—it would just mean that the rig was not going to find any oil. But Lake Peigneur wasn't sitting on an oil reserve—or, at least, not *only* on an oil reserve. About 1,400 feet below the surface of Lake Peigneur was the third level of a salt mine operated by the Diamond Crystal Salt Company. And the hole the oil rig created let the lake's water right into the mine's ceiling.

If you've ever added salt to water, you know that the two mix very well—the salt dissolves, and pretty quickly. And if you're operating a large-scale salt mine, it is a very, very bad thing to have an entire lake—2.5 billion gallons of water, in this case—start flowing in through a crack in a ceiling. This is especially true in the above case, because the salt mine in question (and pragmatically, this makes sense for most salt mines) used salt pillars to support the ceilings against the weight of the levels above. When the water comes rushing in, everything collapses. Everything—including 150-foot oil rigs.

Within minutes, a whirlpool formed at the surface of Lake Peigneur as the water drained into the mine. The whirlpool began sucking everything in the lake into its ever-increasing vortex. Down went the drilling rig and its platform; a dozen boats, many of which were barges carrying things such as trucks; and, perhaps most incredibly, sixty-five acres of land, including an entire island. Delcambre Canal, which before that day was the lake's outlet (ultimately) to the Gulf of Mexico, reversed course, bringing saltwater from the Gulf into the lake. For a few days, the reversed water flow created a 150-foot waterfall—easily the tallest in Louisiana at the time. When the bottom finally finished falling out of Lake Peigneur, the sixty-year-old salt mine was gone, and the once-shallow freshwater lake was now a saltwater basin with a maximum depth of 200 feet.

Amazingly, the death toll from the Lake Peigneur disaster was zero. The fifty-five salt mine workers and all the people on the rig and in boats managed to evacuate in time.

BONUS FACT

Salt and oil have a long history. Edwin Drake, credited with being the first American to successfully drill for oil (at the time to be used for lamps, as whale oil had become expensive), was hired to explore the area beneath Titusville, Pennsylvania, in 1858. But looking for oil dozens of feet below the surface was a new challenge (and a speculative one at that—whether oil could be found and extracted at the depth were both unknown). Drake had decided to simply copy the well-established methods of drilling for salt and apply that idea to oil exploration. He also added a cast-iron pipe to allow him to drill through bedrock without water seeping into the drilling area. With this innovation, the salt-drilling method became the standard for early oil rigs.

EVERYONE'S TEA TIME
WHY IT TAKES A DAM TO MAKE BRITAIN HAPPY

Tea drinking is a cultural touchstone of Great Britain and has been for centuries. Over the years, the traditional stovetop teakettle has fallen from favor, with the electric kettle—which plugs into the wall and heats up much more quickly—taking its place. In general, the electric kettle has few downsides relative to its predecessor.

Unless there's something important on TV.

On July 4, 1990, England and Germany confronted one another in the semifinals of the FIFA World Cup, the quadrennial soccer tournament. The winner would face off against Argentina in the finals; the loser went to the consolation/third-place match against host Italy. At the end of regulation and extra-time, the two countries were tied, 1–1. The match went to a penalty kick shootout, and England's fans sat on the edges of their seats watching.

Germany prevailed, disappointing millions of British. And many sought solace—a bit of it, at least—in a fresh cup of tea. So they took to the electric kettles, turning on approximately a million of them, all within a few minutes of each other. Suddenly, the British National Grid—the electricity network—was being asked to provide a massive amount of power, all on a moment's notice.

This phenomenon, called a "TV pickup," is unique to the United Kingdom. More than 2,500 megawatts of additional power may be needed—that's roughly the equivalent of firing up three nuclear power plants, to capacity, immediately. And, according to the BBC, to time the need properly, an engineer at the National Grid Control Centre is assigned to watch TV. Some of the most popular shows, such as the soap opera *EastEnders* (and of course, soccer matches) do not end at a specific time, as the BBC at times fails to adhere to its schedule.

To compensate for the tea-driven energy needs, the UK has two on-demand power sources. First, France has provided as much as 600 MW of power at times. And second, there's the Dinorwig Power Station in North Wales, a hydroelectric plant. Dinorwig, typically, is idle, and therefore produces no electrical output. But when needed, the water stored in the reservoir above it is released, allowing the power station to produce up to 1,800 MW in roughly sixteen seconds (so says Wikipedia). Combined with other at-the-ready power plants, the National Grid has been able to mostly handle the nationwide impromptu tea times.

Television-viewing habits gave the phenomenon its name, but the National Grid has to prepare for other situations—and in one case, more so than at any other time. The World Cup match required an additional 2,800 MW of power, a television-related record. But on August 11, 1999, the grid requirements surged by 3,000 MW. The cause? The first visible solar eclipse in nearly seventy-five years.

BONUS FACT

Turning off power seems like a great way to save energy, but there are exceptions. In 2007, organizers of both the UK's "Live Earth" concert and the BBC's "Planet Earth" celebration wanted to get British citizens to participate in what they called the "big switch-off." Everyone would be encouraged to simultaneously power down to symbolically demonstrate energy conservation needs. The National Grid objected, noting that the "switch-off" may have actually created environmental harm. As reported by the BBC, the experts at the Grid reasoned that "the unpredictability of demand during such an event could mean some people losing their electricity supply and even raise the danger of emitting more carbon dioxide rather than less."

DEEP IN THE HEART
OF WARTIME
THE BRITISH BAN ON CLAPPING

The American singer Perry Como, beginning in the 1940s and into the 1960s, hosted one of the first musical variety shows on television. But before he took to the airwaves, he performed as part of a traveling orchestra led by Ted Weems, who himself helped establish the big band genre. Together, Como and the Weems Orchestra recorded nearly two dozen songs in the late 1930s and the early 1940s. One of those songs was "Deep in the Heart of Texas," recorded on December 9, 1941, just two days after the Japanese bombed Pearl Harbor.

Although those two events—the recording of a song about Texas and an attack on Hawaii—seem entirely unrelated, as it turns out, the song played a role in the war effort. But not in Texas, and, for that matter, not in Hawaii. "Deep in the Heart of Texas" became a song of note in Great Britain.

The song is a simple tune lasting just under two minutes. It contains five stanzas, each featuring a pair of items ("The stars at night are big and bright" and "The prairie sky is wide and high" in the first stanza) that are found "deep in the heart of Texas," as one could easily guess. However the song isn't known for its lyrics, but rather, the clapping. Before singing "deep in the heart of Texas" each of the ten times one finds it in the song, Como and the orchestra clapped four times. The evocative clapping became the song's hallmark, as it invited participation from the audience.

The anthem rose to popularity quickly, even outside of Texas. It topped the charts of the U.S. television and radio program *Your Hit Parade* for five weeks and then went global, gaining traction in the United Kingdom. Bing Crosby covered the song, recording his own version in 1942, which hit number three on the *Billboard* charts. This version earned a lot of radio play on the BBC and became a favorite of factory workers. Many would momentarily stop their jobs to join in—clap clap clap clap—for the two minutes that the song took over the airwaves.

Which is why it became a problem.

In 2008, the *Guardian* newspaper revisited this moment in British history. As the paper noted, the British government did not take kindly to wartime workers taking impromptu breaks due to what they heard on the radio, so it took action. The BBC ruled that "Deep in the Heart of Texas" was not allowed to be broadcast "on programs that might be heard by factory workers, who might neglect their lathes to join in the song's clapping routine." The ban was lifted before the war ended.

BONUS FACT

In August 1962, American singer Bobby "Boris" Pickett released the Halloween novelty song "Monster Mash" and found solid success. The song—his only hit—reached the top of the U.S. *Billboard* chart on October 20 of that year. But it took more than a decade to reach similar success in the UK. Why? Because in 1962, the BBC banned the song from the airwaves, claiming it was "too morbid." When the song was re-released in 1973, the BBC changed its tune, and "Monster Mash" rose to number three on the UK charts.

THE SENTENCE OF
ONE HAND CLAPPING
A DESPOT'S NONSENSICAL WAYS TO KEEP POWER

European history has its fair share of dictators, but since the fall
of the Iron Curtain, almost all of the continent's nations have
established more freedom-friendly governments. The lone exception is Alexander Lukashenko, the President of Belarus, who once
described himself to Reuters (correctly) as "the last and only dictator in Europe." And since 1994, Lukashenko has ruled Belarus by
force or guile, as one would expect any dictator to do. When he
won re-election in 2010—under questionable voting conditions, to
say the least—thousands took to the streets of Minsk in protest.
More than 700 people were arrested (including a half-dozen people
who, just a few days earlier, were presidential candidates), and a few
people were charged with crimes carrying fifteen-year prison sentences. Lukashenko's message was clear: Dissent won't be tolerated.

Although most protesters have stayed away, a handful—several
hundreds—found a way to passively protest without placards, chants,
or any words whatsoever. As the *Economist* reported in July 2011,
every Wednesday the group started appearing in the streets, wherever they were in Belarus, and began clapping. The clapping protests,
organized via social networks, caught the attention of the rank and

file Belarusian and, of course, of Lukashenko. His response? He hired enforcers to drive around in vans and arrest people, quite literally, for clapping in the streets.

Over the course of a few weeks, according to the *Christian Science Monitor*, more than 1,700 people were arrested. One of the people nabbed was a man named Konstantin Kaplin. He, like the others, was convicted of the crime of applauding in public. Many of his fellow convicts received very strict sentences—fifteen days in prison and "hefty fines," per the *CSM*.

Kaplin asserted that he was innocent. He claimed that he wasn't protesting, but watching, taking pictures of the actual protesters on his cell phone camera. Rather, he argued, this was a case of being in the wrong place at the wrong time. Others certainly made similar arguments, but Kaplin could produce incontrovertible evidence that he wasn't there clapping up a storm.

His proof? He has only one arm.

Unfortunately, the Belarusian police, being subordinate to a dictator with a history of dealing unkindly with insubordination, testified otherwise. Kaplin, despite missing an arm and the requisite attached hand needed to clap, was, they said, still clapping. The Belarusian judge, in the same situation as the police officers, convicted the one-armed "clapper."

The sentence, fortunately, was softer than the typical one, with no time served and only a fine of $200. But for Kaplin, it was still significant. Because he was a pensioner, the fine was equal to twice his monthly grant from the state.

BONUS FACT

Insulting President Lukashenko is a crime in Belarus, punishable by up to five years in prison.

THE MAN WITH
THE GOLDEN ARM
WHO ALSO SAVED MILLIONS OF LIVES

In the mid-1940s, an Australian teenager named James Harrison lost a lung to metastasized pneumonia. The procedure to remove the lung required major blood transfusions, thirteen liters in total. Harrison spent three months in the hospital recovering, and even at that young age, he understood that the extraordinary number of transfusions was fundamental in saving his life. He vowed that, as an adult, he would repay the favor and become a blood donor himself.

Through 2012, Harrison has fulfilled that promise—a thousand times over.

In 1954, soon after he began fulfilling his promise, researchers noticed something unusual about his blood. It contained a rare antibody, one that could unlock a cure for a disease that affects fetuses. The illness is called Rhesus disease, named after a protein also found in the blood of Rhesus monkeys. The protein, in and of itself, is typically not an issue for day-to-day lives; a person can be "Rh+" (that is, has the protein) or "Rh-" and, generally, not know or care.

But when a woman becomes pregnant, the presence of the Rhesus protein comes into play. If the mother is Rh- and the fetus inherits Rh+ blood from the father, the mother's immune system may end up attacking the fetus's bloodstream, seeing it as a threat. This can result in a wide range of medical complications for the fetus, ranging from being mildly anemic at birth to being stillborn.

Before discovering Harrison, doctors believed that the right type of antibody could be used to create a vaccine against Rhesus disease. Harrison had that antibody. Researchers asked him to undergo a series of tests to see if his blood could provide the cure and, after he obtained a $1 million life insurance policy to protect his wife in case anything went wrong, Harrison agreed.

Harrison's blood provided the key to beating the disease. His blood plasma contained an extremely rare antibody, which was used to develop something called the Anti-D vaccine. This suppresses the Rh- mother's immune system from attacking Rh+blood.

Since discovering that his bloodstream contains a life-saving ingredient, Harrison has been on a mission to make the most of it. He has donated plasma, on average, about eighteen times a year—roughly once every three weeks—since 1954. In May 2011, he made his 1,000th donation, easily a record. Each donation takes about forty minutes—that's just under a month of his life dedicated to giving blood.

From the world's perspective, that's certainly a great deal. To date, hundreds of thousands of women—including his own daughter—have received the vaccine made from Harrison's blood. In total, Harrison's antibody has been used to treat more than 2 million babies who would otherwise have Rhesus disease. And millions more in the future will be saved by the antibody that he and others naturally produce.

BONUS FACT

In around 2002, an Australian nine-year-old named Demi-Lee Brennan lost her liver to a virus. She received a transplant from a twelve-year-old only a day or two later, saving her life. For some reason, her body adopted the donor's blood type as her own, changing it from O-negative to O-positive, as reported by the *Sydney Morning Herald*. Typically, organ transplant recipients require immunosuppressive drugs to prevent their bodies from rejecting new organs, as their bodies treat the life-saving additions as foreign invaders. But Brennan's case was different. She not only adopted the donor's blood type, but also his immune system. Hers is the only known case of such a phenomenon.

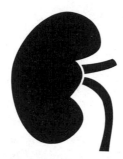

DE GROTE DONORSHOW
THE WORLD'S STRANGEST—
AND BEST—REALITY TV SHOW

People typically come with two healthy kidneys. We only need one in order to survive, and therefore the second one can be donated without much risk to the donor. In general, the procedure to donate a kidney is no more dangerous than any other surgery, although—being a surgical procedure—it is not without risk. Typically, kidneys fail in tandem (although in rare cases, most often caused by blunt trauma or cancer, only one will). Therefore, leaving yourself with only one kidney isn't as risky as many would believe—if it fails, most likely, the other would have as well.

Due to moral and practical concerns (which are subjects for other publications), selling one's kidney is illegal in most of the world. In the United States, for example, in 2011, *CBS News* reported that a New Jersey man was sentenced to two and a half years in prison for brokering kidney sales. Given the political and legal restraints upon transactions regarding kidneys and other organs, people have come up with many creative solutions. For example, a recent pair of Nobel laureates in Economics earned the award for their work in "matching theory"—which, as *The New York Times* noted, can be used to link up kidney donors and donees who otherwise do not know each other.

And where there is room for a Nobel Prize, there's probably room for its polar opposite: reality TV. As *Mental Floss* notes, a Dutch television producer came up with a shocking concept: a show in which three patients, each in need of a kidney, present their cases to the audience. Waiting in the wings is a terminally ill patient with a kidney, ready for donation upon her death, to be given to whomever the viewers at home deem the most worthy. The 2007 show, called *De Grote Donorshow*, was, to say the least, controversial. There were attempts to censor it. The Dutch Kidney Foundation asked the show to remove their logo from it, and many officials decried the show as reflecting poorly on the Netherlands.

But the outrage was, it turns out, unwarranted. *De Grote Donorshow* was a sham. It was designed to raise awareness of the lack of available kidneys in the Netherlands and the country's low rate of organ donor registration. The terminally ill patient was a model/actress; no kidney would be donated. The three patients in renal failure did, in fact, need kidneys, but they were in on the ruse. The deception worked. Per the Dutch news portal NU.nl, just days after the finale aired, more than 40,000 donor forms were downloaded off the national donor registry's website, and within a month or so, over 7,000 new donors registered.

BONUS FACT

According to *The Wall Street Journal*, "only one country . . . has eliminated the shortage of transplant organs." That country? Iran. How? Via "a working and legal payment system for organ donation." Iranian donors can get in excess of $5,000 for a kidney, part from the government and the rest from a nonprofit organization designed to facilitate donations. (For some perspective, the per capita GDP of the United States is about $48,000; Iran's is about $6,000.)

DONOR 150
HOW CHILDREN OF SPERM DONORS FIND THEIR HALF-SIBLINGS

Starting in the late 1980s, a man six feet three inches tall, weighing 163 pounds, with blond hair and blue eyes, himself born in Wilmington, Delaware, started donating sperm. In doing so, he helped create at least a dozen children. As these children's mothers are scattered all over the country, the children are as well. And in most cases, these biological half-siblings have never met each other.

But some of the children of this man—Donor 150 of the California Cryobank—have connected. On Sunday, November 20, 2005, *The New York Times* ran a story titled, "Hello, I'm Your Sister. Our Father is Donor 150." It recounted how two of the girls—Danielle Pagano, then a sixteen-year-old from Long Island, New York, and JoEllen Marsh, then a fifteen-year-old from northwestern Pennsylvania—connected. Connecting with their father, though, seemed like a stretch. As the *Times* noted, "Like most anonymous sperm donors, Donor 150 of the California Cryobank will probably never meet any of the offspring he fathered through sperm bank donations." The donees never knew his true identity, making it intentionally impossible for them or their progeny to contact the donor-dad.

But finding a half-sibling is a different story. Many donee-parents sign up to work with an organization called the Donor Sibling Registry, which operates a database of children associated with their donors' information. That information is scant, but it has enough to connect half-siblings—all you need to know is what sperm bank the sperm came from and the donor's anonymous identification number, which the donee-moms have. From its founding in 2000 through 2012, the Donor Sibling Registry has successfully connected nearly 10,000 half-siblings born from donors.

In the case noted above, soon after these two found each other, other half-siblings followed suit. A group of them planned have a family "reunion" (a misnomer, as they'd never met) that Thanksgiving. Due to the coverage from the article, this scattered pseudo-family grew, as other half-siblings connected as well.

Another person who came across the article? Jeffrey Harrison, a vagabond of sorts, who, per the *Times*, had a checkered history. The *Times* called him "a gentle and kindhearted man" who "liked yoga and animals, lived in an R.V., [had] posed for *Playgirl* during his sperm-donor days, was an unabashed believer in a host of conspiracy theories and supported himself and his small menagerie with odd jobs." He happened across that day's paper in the discard pile at a cafe he frequented in Venice, California. Finding the paper in the cafe was a stroke of luck—the *Sunday Times*, especially in parts of the country other than New York, doesn't last very long, and typically, when it was deposited in the used bin at the cafe, it lacked the front section.

But Jeffrey Harrison was not one of Pagano or Marsh's siblings. He, better known as Donor 150, was their biological father.

To date, Harrison has a mixed relationship with his offspring, whom he often stops by to visit as he travels around in his RV. Some treat him as a "fun uncle," in his words, who makes seemingly random appearances in their lives. Marsh sees him as someone who wants to be "more than just a donor." Others don't envision a permanent role in their lives for Harrison. But most are appreciative of the fact that their previously unknown genetic history is no longer a specter.

BONUS FACT

Starting in 2005, sperm donors in the United Kingdom could no longer donate anonymously. This led to a significant drop in the amount of sperm available, and UK women wanting donors turned elsewhere— most often to Denmark, whose sperm donation laws have become less stringent during the same time period. The BBC and *The Sun* newspaper report that the Danish sperm bank Cryos (which pays donors) has become so popular in recent years that it now claims to export sperm to 60 different nations and has enough stored on hand for well over 10,000 inseminations. As of 2011, the waiting list to donate sperm at Cryos was more than 500 people long, and it's not first-come, first-served (pardon the crude and unintentional pun). Cryos can be selective. It no longer accepts donations from redheads, citing a lack of demand.

PAIN IN THE RED
HOW HAIR AND PAIN ARE, PROBABLY, LINKED

Approximately 1–2 percent of the world's population has red hair, with the majority of such people coming from European descent. Roughly 12 percent of Scots and 10 percent of Irish people are believed to have red hair, well above the populations of other countries. Being a redhead typically goes along with a fair complexion and freckles. But it may come with something else as well—a resistance to anesthesia.

Red hair is genetic. Those with it have two recessive genes that cause a mutation of a gene called the "melanocortin 1 receptor," or MC1R for short. The MC1R gene determines, in part, what type of melanin our bodies produce, and melanin, ultimately, gives us our hair, skin, and eye color. In the case of redheads, the MC1R mutation causes a lower production of eumelanin, the type of melanin that causes darker features, and an increased amount of pheomelanin, which, well, doesn't. The MC1R mutation also probably leads to freckles and increased sensitivity to ultraviolet light.

It may also have something to do with one's ability to tolerate pain.

Anecdotally, many stories tell of redheads disproportionately avoiding painful medical and dental procedures, and of doctors and dentists giving redheads more anesthesia than darker-haired people. In 2009, the *Journal of the American Dental Association* published a paper investigating whether redheads avoided the dentist disproportionately. Twice as many redheads—compared to people with black or brown hair—admitted doing so due to fear of pain and ineffective Novocain.

In 2005, a team of researchers from the University of Louisville took the investigation further, hoping to see if the fear had a basis in reason. The team exposed a test group to "thermal pain"—pain induced by excessive cold or heat—and published their findings in the medical journal *Anesthesiology*. They concluded that redheads were indeed more sensitive to such pain, and had a natural resistance to subcutaneous lidocaine, an anesthetic.

The *Anesthesiology* article wasn't an outlier. In 2010, the *Scandinavian Journal of Pain* published a paper with similar findings; in that case, twenty redheads, all female, required more capsaicin—a topical anesthesia—in order to get the same effect as the twenty blonds/dark-haired women in the study. In general, the scientific community believes that people with the MC1R mutation that causes red hair require 20 percent more anesthesia than typical, in order to achieve the same effect. And because a lot of practitioners don't realize this, redheads unfortunately experience more pain at the hands of dentists and doctors than they would otherwise. As one doctor told *The New York Times*, the cure is simple: Redheads should tell their doctors about this little quirk of genetics.

BONUS FACT

If you're in the United States, and you go to the dentist to get a cavity filled, the dentist will probably ask you if you want some

Novocain. But that's not what you're getting. Novocain is rarely used because lidocaine is more effective and hypoallergenic. According to WebMD's reference guide Medscape, procaine (the generic name for Novocain)—brand or generic—has been discontinued from the U.S. market. Dentists often use the term "Novocain" anyway as that is the term patients are, incorrectly it turns out, familiar with.

RED LIGHT, GREEN LIGHT
NORTH KOREA'S HUMAN-POWERED TRAFFIC LIGHTS

North Korea is, in many ways, living in the Dark Ages. Things Westerners take for granted, such as on-demand electricity, are notably lacking. Private car ownership is almost entirely unheard of—as of 1990 there were only about a quarter of a million cars in the country as a whole, and most of them, by a large margin, were owned by the military. Only about 1,000 miles of paved roads exist, and the purchase of fuel is extremely restricted. So there are not a lot of cars on the roads—and even in places with relatively heavy traffic, the lack of infrastructure means no traffic lights.

But no traffic lights would mean more traffic accidents, and that would be a very bad thing. The solution? Young women trained to direct traffic and stationed atop umbrella-adorned platforms in the middle of intersections.

Each Pyongyong traffic controller wears a navy blue suit with a white pilot hat and sturdy black shoes, the last of which makes sense given that these women spend their working days on their feet, rotating and pivoting for hours at a time. The traffic controllers—all female—are trained to be robotic and purposeful with their movements. Each action is crisp and exact, and the traffic controller only rotates counter-clockwise, directing traffic with nothing more than a baton and a whistle. (You may have to see it to believe it, and you can find videos of these robotic ladies on YouTube.)

Think this is another example of the insanity that is North Korea? You're probably right—but it gets stranger. These female traffic controllers have been around since the 1970s but the platforms that shield them from the sun or rain are relatively new. North Korea's state-run media agency, the Korean Central News Agency, reported on the addition of these platforms in 1998. The report has the markings of the dictatorial nation's obsession with propaganda over truth, noting that "[t]he traffic controllers are moved by the warm affection shown for them by General Secretary Kim Jong Il who saw to it that the platforms with umbrellas are being set up this time after raincoats, rain boots, sunglasses, gloves and cosmetics as well as seasonal uniforms were provided to them."

BONUS FACT

As ridiculous as the North Korean traffic solution is, it does, perhaps, solve one real problem—colorblind motorists who have trouble with traffic lights. Other countries have come up with less ridiculous solutions, such as a traffic light with different shapes for each color—a (red) square means stop, a (yellow) diamond means slow down, and a (green) circle means go.

FANDEMONIUM
THE KILLER IN YOUR BEDROOMS?

Travel to South Korea and purchase a regular, vanilla, oscillating fan. Plug it in and let it cool the room you are in. An hour or two later, max, you will most likely have to turn it back on. Chances are, the fan will have turned off automatically. Why? Because, as recently as 2006, the Korea Consumer Protection Board (KCPB) believed that falling asleep with a fan running can lead to death.

On July 18, 2006, the KCPB issued a consumer advisory that asserted the following:

> If bodies are exposed to electric fans or air conditioners for too long, it causes bodies to lose water and hypothermia. If directly in contact with a fan, could lead to death from increase of carbon dioxide saturation concentration and decrease of oxygen concentration. The risks are higher for the elderly and patients with respiratory problems.
>
> From 2003–2005, a total of 20 cases were reported through the CISS involving asphyxiations caused by leaving electric fans and air conditioners on while sleeping. To prevent asphyxiation, timers should be set, wind direction should be rotated and doors should be left open.

"Fan death," as it is called, is a commonly believed myth in South Korea. It is so common, in fact, that some South Koreans who moved to the United States to attend college admitted to believing the myth until well after they arrived in the States. And the Korean Wikipedia entry for fan death does not call it a myth but rather "controversial."

But "fan death," of course, is patently false. A leading expert on hypothermia, Gordon Giesbrecht of the University of Manitoba, went to the Korean press to debunk this assertion: "It's hard to imagine, because to die of hypothermia, [one's body temperature] would have to get down to 28 [degrees Celsius], drop by 10 degrees overnight. We've got people lying in snow banks overnight here in Winnipeg and they survive . . . Someone is not going to die from hypothermia because their body temperature drops two or three degrees overnight; it would have to drop eight to 10 degrees."

Yet the myth—which has unknown origins and no scientific basis—continues to be widely accepted in South Korea to this day.

BONUS FACT

According to a study published in a 2008 issue of the *Archives of Pediatric & Adolescent Medicine*, infants who sleep in rooms with fans running may have a *lower* incidence of Sudden Infant Death Syndrome than those who do not.

FANS AND PEANUTS
WHY "TAKE ME OUT TO THE BALLGAME" IS A LIE

For over a century, baseball games have taken an elongated pause after the away team's half of the seventh inning, in a tradition long known as the "seventh inning stretch." Many Major League Baseball teams have traditions specific to their stadiums for this break. The New York Mets sing "Lazy Mary" and throw T-shirts into the stands. The Cincinnati Reds sing "Twist and Shout" and the Toronto Blue Jays lead fans in stretching exercises. But one tradition spans all thirty ballparks: a sing-along of "Take Me Out to the Ballgame."

In the late nineteenth century and into the twentieth, popular American music was dominated by a group of composers and lyricists who worked primarily with sheet music publishers located on West 28th Street between Fifth and Sixth Avenues in Manhattan. That street, known as Tin Pan Alley, featured household names such as George and Ira Gershwin as well as Irving Berlin, and produced "God Bless America," "Sweet Georgia Brown," and other songs that have withstood the test of time. "Take Me Out to the Ballgame" was one of them, written in 1908 by two men named Jack Norworth and Albert Von Tilzer. The song they penned told of a young woman named Katie Casey who, as we learn in the first stanza, "was baseball mad" and attended every game she could afford. Her love of the game was so deep that "on a Saturday her young beau // called to see if she'd like go // to see a show, but Miss Kate said 'No,'" because she wanted to go to a ballgame instead. The chorus is Katie Casey's request that her gentleman caller take her to see a baseball game.

But Misters Norworth and Von Tilzer didn't share Miss Kate's love of the game. Although Katie Casey never missed a game, Norworth and Von Tilzer missed them all. Prior to writing "Take Me Out to the Ballgame," neither of them had ever attended a baseball game.

Norworth, the lyricist, was (clearly) not inspired by the crowd nor the peanuts and Cracker Jacks. While he was riding the New York City subway one day, a sign reading "Baseball Today—Polo Grounds" caught his eye, and inspiration took hold. Von Tilzer set it to music, and a few decades later—no one is certain how, or when—the song became the in-game staple. Yet the pair weren't fans of the game to which they gave such a gift. Von Tilzer wouldn't attend his first Major League game until the 1920s and Norworth attended his first one in 1940.

Whether either of the pair was a fan of peanuts and/or Cracker Jacks is, to this day, unknown.

BONUS FACT

We don't know where or when the "Take Me Out to the Ballgame" seventh-inning sing-along began, but one early example—perhaps the one that popularized it—was the result of a prank. In the 1970s, famed baseball broadcaster Harry Caray, then a play-by-play announcer for the White Sox, was known to sing along to the song while in the broadcast booth, but with his microphone off. Bill Veeck found out about this and one day—unbeknownst to Caray—he turned the broadcaster's microphone on and piped Caray's rendition to the fans. The fans loved it, and when Caray moved to the crosstown Cubs, he kept it up.

KILLING CHARLOTTE BRAUN
THE LOST PEANUTS *CHARACTER*

Peanuts, the iconic comic strip, debuted on October 2, 1950. In the first strip—four frames—Charlie Brown walks past two other children, Shermy and Patty (the latter being a character distinct from Peppermint Patty, who didn't join the cast until the mid 1960s), as the two gossip behind his back. A few days later, the strip's creator, Charles Schulz, introduced Snoopy to the world, and over the next decade, Lucy, Linus, Schroeder, and many others joined the cast of characters. The vast majority of them were well liked for the nearly fifty-year run of the strip.

The exception? Charlotte Braun, who debuted on November 30, 1954, and was intended to be the female counterpart to Charlie Brown. (This becomes obviously true if you say both characters' names aloud.) Before the next spring, Braun made her final appearance in *Peanuts*. In one sense, she was killed by a woman named Elizabeth Swain.

Swain wasn't a character in *Peanuts*, though. She was a fan—one, who, like many other *Peanuts* fans, did not take well to Braun. The character was abrasive, loud, and didn't have many friends in the fan community. As Henry L. Katz, a curator of popular graphic art at the Library of Congress would tell *ABC News*, the character was "a little too serious" and "didn't have the warmth or the humor of the other characters." In short, nobody liked Charlotte Braun.

Fans wrote letters to Schulz, objecting to the inclusion of Braun, and in one case Schulz wrote back. Elizabeth Swain—then in her early twenties—received a letter from the noted cartoonist dated January 5, 1955. Schulz wrote:

> I am taking your suggestion regarding Charlotte Braun and will eventually discard her. If she appears anymore it will be in strips that were already completed before I got your letter or because someone writes in saying that they like her. Remember, however, that you and your friends will have the death of an innocent child on your conscience. Are you prepared to accept such responsibility?
>
> Thanks for writing, and I hope that future releases will please you.

At the bottom, Schulz doodled a picture of Charlotte Braun, grimacing, with an axe buried in her head.

Swain, who would go on to become a research librarian, passed away in 2000, a few months after Schulz. She donated the letter to the Library of Congress (which, coincidentally, she worked for early in her career).

As for Charlotte Braun, she didn't "die" on that day in January. She lasted a few more weeks. She appeared for the last time in the *Peanuts* strip on February 1, 1955, and Lucy inherited her brash, loud-voiced style.

BONUS FACT

The name *Peanuts* has nothing to do with Schulz's vision for the strip. Schulz wanted to retain the name of his predecessor comic, *Li'l*

Folks, but his syndicate thought the name was confusingly similar to the already popular *Li'l Abner*. The syndicate, not Schulz, decided on *Peanuts*, a reference to the peanut gallery on the *Howdy Doody Show*. Schulz's take on the name? In a 1987 interview, he protested: "It's totally ridiculous, has no meaning, is simply confusing, and has no dignity—and I think my humor has dignity."

LUNCH AND A MURDER
THE REAL COLD CASE INVESTIGATORS

Prime-time television has trained us to believe that murder cases are investigated by multiple, highly experienced homicide detectives with access to seemingly endless resources. At their disposal are things such as high-level scientific testing labs able to extract fingerprints and/or DNA from seemingly nothing; machines that can take even the grainiest closed-circuit camera image and give us a perfect depiction of a suspect's full face; and other tools bound only by the show writers' imaginations. Reality, especially for small-town police departments, is very different. Many murders—often brutal ones that are given the full attention of local law enforcement—remain unsolved.

What can police departments like these do? Call Batman? Hardly. But they can call the Vidocq Society.

Founded in 1990, this group of forensic professionals—psychologists and prosecutors, homicide detectives and FBI profilers, scientists and coroners—gathers for lunch monthly in Philadelphia, hoping to give a cold case a fresh lead. The Society is named after Eugène François Vidocq, a French criminal turned vigilante crime fighter—a man who was perhaps the first private detective, and is regarded as the father of modern criminology. It was founded by three men—all of different backgrounds—who met during the course of crime-solving endeavors. Bill Fleisher is the most ordinary of the bunch—an FBI agent. Richard Walter, a forensic psychologist, is one of the forefathers of modern criminal profiling. Finally, the Vidocq Society counts among its cofounders the late Frank Bender, a self-taught sculptor with a particular knack for creating reproductions of people's heads using only their skulls and photos of what they once looked like.

The Society began on a lark. The three had corresponded over the years but only first met, face-to-face, in May 1989. As expected, they began to talk shop, discussing the mysteries they were working on, informally collaborating and helping each other. One suggested that the trio make it a regular event; another suggested inviting other colleagues from across the law enforcement world. According to *The Telegraph*, they sent out twenty-eight invitations expecting only a reply or two. They received twenty-six acceptances, and with that, the Vidocq Society was born.

Each month, the Vidocq Society—at the Society's expense (they pay for travel out of the group's $100/year membership dues)—invites a law enforcement officer to present a cold case over lunch. Two specific requirements apply: The unsolved death has to be at least two years old, and the alleged victim mustn't have been involved in criminal activity such as dealing drugs or prostitution.

To date, they've had some success, helping to solve a handful of crimes over the years, including a 2005 double homicide that made it into the TV show *America's Most Wanted*. And in at least one case—the death of Huey Cox of Little Rock, Arkansas, in 1991—the Society managed to free a wrongfully accused man by demonstrating that the suspect police had charged with the crime was innocent of it.

BONUS FACT

In 1996, the Vidocq Society made an appearance in a Hardy Boys/Nancy Drew mystery, a joint version of the children's novels. The Vidocq story was written by long-time Nancy Drew author Carolyn Keene. Keene—and for that matter, Hardy Boys author Franklin W. Dixon—don't exist, and never have. Both authors are collective pseudonyms, used as a way for the publisher (the Stratemeyer Syndicate originally) to maintain a team of writers (and produce a high volume of books) under a consistent brand.

THE PASSION OF THE MONEY-LAUNDERING EXTORTIONIST
THE OFFICIAL MOVIE OF THE WAR ON DRUGS?

In 2004, Mel Gibson released *The Passion of the Christ*, the controversial movie that he directed and produced. The movie grossed over $600 million at the box office. On May 10, 2012, a man named Jorge Vazquez pleaded guilty to money laundering and extortion. In September, he'd be sentenced to seven years in prison. And as part of the plea deal, the U.S. government received 10 percent of the potential profits from the sequel to *The Passion of the Christ*.

Really.

The Passion of the Christ was written by Gibson and Benedict Fitzgerald, a previously unknown writer. Fitzgerald did not make a lot of money off the film—in a lawsuit he later filed against Gibson, he claimed that he was led to believe that the film would be a small-budget film, leading him to take a relatively small payday for the script—and took a loan to fund future projects. When he defaulted on the loan, he sold his rights to the script he was working on, a sequel to *Passion* called *Mary, Mother of Christ*. The company that bought those rights was owned in part by a San Antonio man named Arturo Madrigal.

Back to Vazquez. When criminals plead guilty to a crime, they need to tell the court what they did wrong; this is called an "allocution." In Vazquez's allocution, he admitted that he and others kidnapped Madrigal's brother in Mexico in an effort to get Madrigal to sign over his rights to the screenplay to *Mary*, which Madrigal did. (Vazquez claimed that Madrigal owed him money and said he was looking for leverage to get his debt repaid.) Vazquez then turned around and sold the script to a production company, receiving $1 million up front and a 10-percent stake in the movie's profits.

According to *MySanAntonio.com*, the plea agreement came with a strange price—the government demanded that Vazquez give up his 10-percent cut of future earnings, with that money going into the Feds' bank account.

Why the government believed that Vazquez had the right to give them those proceeds, is, at best, unclear, given that it was incarcerating Vazquez in part for his method of acquiring the rights. Certainly, Madrigal disagreed that Vazquez had any ownership of the screenplay. On the day Vazquez plead guilty, Madrigal sued Vazquez in an effort to reverse the latter's sale of the script.

BONUS FACT

In recent years, a common Christmastime "prank" sprang up in the United States—thieves began stealing baby Jesus dolls from nativity scenes around the country. According to the Awl, from 2011 to 2012 there were well over 2,000 reports of such thefts. For many, it's no laughing matter. In 2012, the *New York Post* reported that police treated one theft from a Brooklyn church as a hate crime. That same year, according to the *Los Angeles Times,* a Florida church, tired of having its baby Jesus statue stolen, outfitted their new one with a GPS device to catch a future thief.

STOLEN SMILE
THE INCREDIBLE HEIST OF THE MONA LISA

On August 21, 1911, the *Mona Lisa*—Leonardo da Vinci's master-piece—was stolen off the wall of the Louvre, leaving bare the four iron pegs on which it hung. The thief, later identified as then-Louvre employee Vincenzo Peruggia, hid in a closet on Saturday, knowing that the museum would be closed the next day. He emerged from his hiding place on August 21, took the *Mona Lisa* off the wall, discarded its nearly 200 pounds of security devices and decorative frames, and carried the painting under his smock. He walked out the door and into freedom—until, twenty-eight months later, he tried to sell it, and was instead nabbed by the authorities.

Peruggia's motivations, however, are almost certainly not those of the standard art thief, that is, he was not looking to simply (to understate the feat) fence the masterpiece and become an overnight millionaire. Rather, Peruggia was either a nationalist ideologue look-ing to reclaim the artwork on behalf of his native Italy, or, perhaps, a rube to a master criminal in the making.

The former theory is straightforward: Peruggia, an Italian by birth, allegedly believed that the Italian da Vinci's work could only be properly displayed in Italy—so he stole it to fix that "problem."

Unfortunately, there are a lot of reasons to believe that Peruggia simply used this excuse—successfully, it turned out—to limit his jail time once caught. (Tried in Italy, he served seven months, with *Time* implying that his patriotic motives played into his short amount of time behind bars.) Some reasons not to believe Peruggia include the fact that he attempted to sell the painting (for the equivalent of $100,000) and not merely donate it; that he waited more than two years to move it; that he returned to France after his release; and that he was at least loosely affiliated with another criminal syndicate of art counterfeiters.

It is the art counterfeiters' story that suggests that Peruggia's motives were less honorable than patriotism.

An Argentine con man named Eduardo de Valfierno allegedly was behind the theft. In 1914, after the theft and recovery of the *Mona Lisa*, but before Peruggia was brought to trial, Valfierno told his story to an American journalist named Karl Decker after extracting a promise that Decker would not publish the story until after Valfierno's death. Decker agreed. This is the only source for Valfierno's account.

Valfierno's "business" was in faux masterpieces. He commissioned artists to create realistic-looking copies of famous works of art and sold them to collectors around the world, claiming the works were original. To buttress his claims of authenticity, he passed off other forgeries—documents from the museums in which the originals hung, stating that the originals had been stolen and, to avoid embarrassment, the museums instead quietly displayed replicas. Unfortunately for Valfierno, one such collector bragged about one of his purchases, leading to press coverage of the (faked) theft—and almost exposing Valfierno's fraud. So Valfierno decided to take no further chances.

As the story goes, Valfierno hired Peruggia and others to steal the *Mona Lisa*—but not before he commissioned the creation of six counterfeits and made sure they were distributed around the United

States. (Valfierno surmised that it would be easy to get through customs before the theft but nearly impossible afterward.) Once the media took up the story of the theft itself, Valfierno was able to sell the six fake paintings without much trouble—and without much risk, as the purchasers, now knowingly buying stolen property, had no real recourse if they ever caught on to the swindle. With the real *Mona Lisa* in Valfierno's possession, he also had the luxury of knowing that the Louvre would never get back the original, making it unlikely at best that the purchasers of the fakes would catch on, anyway. Of course, this part of the scheme did not go according to plan.

Valfierno claims that Peruggia was well compensated for his role, but that the thief gambled the money away. Peruggia's solution? He knew where Valfierno kept the true *Mona Lisa*, so he simply did what he had done a year or two earlier. He stole it. Again.

BONUS FACT

The *Mona Lisa* is not painted on canvas, but on three pieces of wood roughly an inch and a half thick.

UNVANDALISM
VANDALS WHO SAVE ART FROM ITSELF

Originally a church, the Panthéon is now a mausoleum in Paris. Building started in 1758 and was completed in 1790. It is the final resting place of Voltaire, Louis Braille, Victor Hugo, Alexandre Dumas, Marie Curie, and others. Modeled after the building of the same name in Rome, it contains large columns, a dome, and—of unique relevance to the following discussion—a clock. The clock, a relic from the 1800s, stopped chiming in the 1960s when rust overtook its gears, bringing it to a halt.

All that changed in 2006. That year, after an eight-month restoration project, the clock was fixed. But its repair was not due to some public works project nor funded by some fabulously wealthy patron of the arts—at least not outwardly. It was done, surreptitiously, by a group of underground art restorers, cultural preservation advocates, and, perhaps, criminals. The group, which is still around, is called Urban eXperiment, or UX for short.

The history of the UX is murky, but according to Wired, its beginnings stem from a theft three decades ago. A group of teenagers managed to steal a set of maps detailing the series of tunnels running beneath much of Paris—tunnels that provide clandestine access to many Parisian landmarks. Rumor has it that some of these teenagers ended up starting UX, and the maps have become a key way for these pseudo-criminals to avoid detection during repair jobs.

In 2005, a subset of UX called Untergunther used the maps to enter the Panthéon in hopes of restoring the clock in question. Then, they created a secret workshop in the landmark, in a room just below the dome, and got to work. For eight months and at the expense of $10,000 in member-donated monies (their time was uncompensated), the group secretly toiled to repair the long-broken clock. They avoided guards without much effort; the floor where they set up shop was rarely frequented, even by security personnel. They even grew a small vegetable garden on the terrace outside their makeshift workshop.

When they completed the restoration, a new challenge arose. The clock was in working order but needed the Panthéon's staff to maintain it—which, unfortunately, would require telling the staff that the clock had been fixed. This proved incredibly difficult and came at a price, as recounted by *Wired*:

> They notified the director, Bernard Jeannot, by phone, then offered to elaborate in person. Four of them came—two men and two women, including Kunstmann and the restoration group's leader, a woman in her forties who works as a photographer—and were startled when Jeannot refused to believe their story. They were even more shocked when, after they showed him their workshop ("I think I need to sit down," he murmured), the administration later decided to sue UX, at one point seeking up to a year of jail time and 48,300 euros in damages. Jeannot's then-deputy, Pascal Monnet, is now the Panthéon's director, and he has gone so far as to hire a clockmaker to restore the clock to its previous condition by resabotaging it. But the clockmaker refused to do more than disengage a part—the escape wheel, the very part that had been sabotaged the first time. UX slipped in shortly thereafter to take the wheel into its own possession, for safekeeping,

in the hope that someday a more enlightened administration will welcome its return.

In the end, some UX members were brought up on criminal charges but, as noted by the *Guardian*, were acquitted. As for the clock? It is, again, stopped. In the Panthéon, the time is, eternally, 10:51.

BONUS FACT

Marie Curie, whose groundbreaking work on radioactivity changed the history of science, is interred in the Panthéon, as noted above. She died in 1934 from aplastic anemia due to her regular exposure to radioactive isotopes. During her research career, she stored the isotopes in a desk drawer along with her papers. To this day, her papers are tainted with radioactivity and are too dangerous to read as one normally would. According to her Wikipedia entry, her documents "are kept in lead-lined boxes, and those who wish to consult them must wear protective clothing."

DOUBLE BONUS!

In 1903, Curie—with her husband Pierre and physicist Henri Becquerel—won the Nobel Prize in Physics for their work with radioactivity. In 1911, Marie Curie herself won the Nobel Prize in Chemistry. To date, she is the only person to win Nobels in two different scientific disciplines.

DISSOLVING MEDALS
HOW TO HIDE NOBEL PRIZES FROM NAZIS

During World War II, Adolf Hitler prohibited the export of gold from Germany. But gold, being valuable and not easily traced, is very difficult to regulate. (Indeed, that is probably where its true value comes from.) Hitler's edict was, in almost all cases, unenforceable.

One exception? Nobel Prize medals.

Before 1980, the medals given by Sweden (all of them except the Nobel Peace Prize—that award is given by Norway) were made of 600 grams of 23-karat gold—and therefore subject to Hitler's export ban. The recipient's name was engraved on the back of the medal, making it clear who might be breaking the law. This proved uniquely dangerous for two physics laureates, Max von Laue (winner, 1914) and James Franck (1925), both Germans. When World War II began, the two entrusted the Bohr Institute in Copenhagen, Denmark (the research institution of fellow physics laureate Neils Bohr) with the safekeeping of their medals, assuming that Nazi soldiers would have otherwise confiscated their prizes. When Nazi troops invaded Denmark, they raided the Institute. Had von Laue's and Franck's medals been discovered, the consequences would most likely have been dire.

Enter Hungarian chemist George de Hevesy, a future Nobel Laureate himself (in chemistry). He, Jewish, had gone to the Institute looking for—and temporarily at least, finding—safe haven from the Nazis. He and Bohr decided that more standard ways of hiding the medals (e.g. burying them) would not suffice, as the risk of harm to von Laue and Franck was too great to chance the medals' discovery. The chemist de Hevesy took more drastic action. He created a solution of aqua regia—a concoction consisting typically of one part nitric acid to three parts hydrochloric acid—so named because it can dissolve two of the "royal" metals, gold and platinum. He placed the medals in the solution, which promptly dissolved them. He then left the gold-bearing aqua regia solution on his laboratory shelf within the Institute, hidden in plain sight as Nazi storm troopers ransacked the Institute.

The plan worked, and von Laue and Franck were safe—as were their awards. The gold remained safely on that shelf, suspended in aqua regia, for the remainder of the war, unnoticed by the German soldiers. When the war ended, de Hevesy precipitated the gold out of the solution, and the Nobel committee recast the medals.

BONUS FACT

Throughout human history (through 2009, at least), humankind has successfully mined roughly 165,000 metric tons of gold. At gold's density, that comes out to about 300,000 cubic feet—a relatively tiny amount. For comparison's sake, all the gold ever mined could be contained by the New York Public Library's Rose Reading Room, which has a volume of approximately 1.2 million cubic feet.

A CITY FIT FOR A KING
COCA-COLA'S BATTLE AGAINST RACISM

The Reverend Dr. Martin Luther King Jr. was born in Atlanta, Georgia, on January 15, 1929. On October 14, 1964, he became the youngest person to ever win the Nobel Peace Prize. His hometown of Atlanta wanted to throw him a party: an interracial banquet, with official invitations going to the city's leaders and titans of industry. The city's mayor, religious leaders from across faiths, a university president, and the publisher of the major area newspaper signed the invites.

Unfortunately, Atlanta was still racially segregated, and although King had many fans, he also had many enemies. Many whites were upset that King had been honored by the Nobel committee; one of the state's senators, Herman Talmadge, expressed his dissatisfaction with the honor, wondering aloud why the committee gave a peace prize to a person who promoted law-breaking. Invitations to the highly exclusive event came back with many more declinations than expected. A *New York Times* report claimed that a well-known (but unidentified) banker in the Atlanta area took to the phones, hoping to convince other whites to abstain from attending the banquet, and certainly others preached the same message.

As the days ticked by, it looked more and more likely that the Dinkler Plaza Hotel—the site of the gala—was going to be rather empty on the evening of the event. Mayor Ivan Allen realized that such a result would be a stain on the city's reputation, both immediately and forevermore. He also knew that it could significantly set back the clock on racial relations in Atlanta. He struggled to find a solution, but then, an unlikely hero stepped in.

Mayor Allen and J. Paul Austin, the chairman and CEO of the Coca-Cola Company, called a meeting of Atlanta's business leaders, and Austin threw down the gauntlet. According to a memoir (*An Easy Burden*) by a former aide to King named Andrew Brown, Austin told those assembled that "it is embarrassing for Coca-Cola to be located in a city that refuses to honor its Nobel Prize winner. We are an international business. The Coca-Cola Company does not need Atlanta. You all need to decide whether Atlanta needs the Coca-Cola Company."

They decided. Within two hours, all the tickets were sold, and interest in the event skyrocketed so much that Martin Luther King, Sr. (yes, the honoree's father) had trouble getting enough tickets for his own use. The Dinkler Plaza was stuffed to the brim with more than 1,500 partygoers, and, perhaps most importantly, the police detail outside had nothing to do. The police were there to combat the hordes of protesters expected to descend upon and disrupt the party—but the threat never materialized.

BONUS FACT

MLK's birthday became a holiday in 1986, but some states were slow to adopt it. It would not be celebrated in all fifty states until 2000, and Mississippi celebrates it in conjunction with the birthday of Confederate General Robert E. Lee, born January 19, 1807.

COLA ENFORCEMENT AGENCY
HOW COKE GETS ITS COKE

In 1886, Atlanta, Georgia, passed a short-lived law prohibiting the sale and/or manufacture of alcohol. In response, a pharmacist named John Pemberton created a faux wine, mixing together fruit flavors with extracts from kola nuts (caffeine) and coca leaves (cocaine). He dispensed it via soda fountains—at the time, carbonated water was believed to have a medicinal benefit—and with that, Coca-Cola was born.

The original Coke formula had a significant amount of cocaine in it, but that was quickly stemmed and, by 1903 or thereabouts, eliminated from the recipe. This was done, in part, because the desired flavor can be extracted from the coca leaves, thereby removing the cocaine, setting the drug aside as a by-product. To this day, Coca-Cola needs coca leaves to make its drinks; as a Coke exec told *The New York Times*, "Ingredients from the coca leaf are used, but there is no cocaine in it and it is all tightly overseen by regulatory authorities."

In fact, the United States (and most other nations) expressly prohibits the sale and trade of coca leaves. In order for Coca-Cola to continue to exist in its current form, the company has a special arrangement with the Drug Enforcement Administration (DEA) allowing Coke to import dried coca leaves from Peru in huge quantities (and to a lesser degree, from Bolivia). The dried coca leaves make their way to a processing plant in Maywood, New Jersey, operated by the Stepan Corporation, a publicly traded chemicals company. The Stepan factory imports roughly 100 metric tons of the leaves each year, stripping the active ingredient—cocaine— from them. The cocaine-free leaves are then shipped off to Coke to turn into syrup, and, ultimately, soda.

What does Stepan do with the cocaine? It goes to the Mallinck-rodt Group, which creates a legal, topical anesthesia called cocaine hydrochloride. Cocaine hydrochloride is used to numb the lining of the mouth, nose, or throat and requires a DEA order form to obtain.

BONUS FACT

Legend has it that Coca-Cola's recipe contains a mystery flavoring, known as the "7X flavor." It is heavily guarded. In early 2011, *This American Life* broadcast an episode discussing a potential early recipe for the drink but almost certainly not the one in use today. (Coke denied that NPR had discovered the true formula.) In that episode, Mark Pendergrast, author of *For God, Country, and Coca-Cola*, an unauthorized history of the company (and beverage), said that "only two people know how to mix the 7X flavoring ingredient" and that "[t]hose two people never travel on the same plane in case it crashes; it's this carefully passed-on secret ritual, and the formula is kept in a bank vault."

MR. ACID
HOW AMERICA GOT ITS LSD

The typical LSD "hit" has about 100 micrograms of the drug in it. At the high end, that means a gram contains about 10,000 doses. A kilogram of LSD has about 10 million hits in it. It should go without saying that a kilo of LSD is a whole lot of acid.

But not for William Leonard Pickard. At his peak, Pickard was producing a kilogram of the stuff every five weeks.

Pickard was born in California in 1945; his father was a lawyer and his mother an expert at the Centers for Disease Control and Prevention (better known as the CDC). He graduated from Purdue University and returned to California to study advanced chemistry, ending up with a high-level position at UCLA's Drug Policy Research Program in the 1980s. How he obtained his knowledge of drugs and drug making is unclear, but we are sure of one thing: He made a whole lot of LSD.

In 1988, Pickard was making LSD at an architectural shop outside San Francisco, when a neighbor called authorities after detecting a foreign odor. The FBI raided what turned out to be Pickard's lab, discovering 200,000 doses of acid and capturing the mastermind on the premises. Pickard was convicted of manufacturing LSD and served a five-year prison sentence.

After his release, Pickard soon returned to bad habits—and multiplied them. With an accomplice named Clyde Apperson (whose role was limited to setting up and taking down acid labs), Pickard traversed the United States, creating temporary LSD labs. He was in Oregon in early 1996, then in Colorado later in that year, and from part of 1997 through most of 1999, in Santa Fe. In his labs, Pickard cranked out absurd amounts of the drug, moving on to another location before neighbors took notice.

Pickard was apprehended in 2000 in Wamego, Kansas, after another accomplice turned informant and assisted the Drug Enforcement Administration (DEA) in apprehending him and Apperson. The informant, Gordon Todd Skinner, advised the DEA that the pair was moving operations to a former missile silo in that town (even though Skinner had actually moved the lab already but not yet informed Pickard or Apperson). The DEA arrested the pair when they attempted to relocate it again, in the back of a Ryder rental truck a few days later.

Per the *Washington Times*, the amount of LSD available in the United States plummeted by 95 percent after Pickard's arrest. He is serving two life sentences in Arizona.

BONUS FACT

The little circles or dots you may "see" when your eyes are closed are hallucinations called phosphenes. Typically, when your eyes are open, light hits your retinas and your eyes' optics work to build a picture of what the eyes are focused on. But the retinas can be stimulated mechanically as well—if something pushes down on them, the pressure will be translated into nonsensical images. When you rub your closed eyes, the pressure creates the images you're experiencing. (This is also why you sometimes see "stars" when you sneeze or get hit in the head.)

HIGH AND OUTSIDE
BASEBALL'S MOST UNLIKELY NO-HITTER

One of the rare feats a Major League Baseball pitcher can accomplish is a no-hitter—a game in which he (or a group of pitchers on his team) prevents the other team from getting even a single hit during a regulation, nine-inning game. From 1875 through 2012, there have been only 272 "no-no"s. The accomplishment takes not only exceptional physical abilities—one has to be able to command multiple pitch types, throw a ball with superhuman velocity, and have pitching mechanics that are near-perfect—but also requires a lot of luck. And given the pressure of the situation, in most cases, pitching a no-hitter also requires mental acuity.

"In most cases" because of a man named Dock Ellis.

Ellis was, as Major League pitchers go, a bit of an odd duck. He took to wearing hair curlers during pregame warmups, and, according to the Baseball Reliquary, only stopped when MLB's commissioner demanded he do so. In 1974, while pitching against the Cincinnati Reds, he hoped to motivate his team by taking aim at the other players—literally. In the first inning alone, he beaned three players (including Pete Rose) before throwing the ball behind Hall of Fame catcher Johnny Bench's head, after which he was promptly removed from the game. As a member of the Texas Rangers in 1977, he famously led a player uprising against his manager, Billy Hunter; Ellis told the AP that "[Hunter] is Hitler but he ain't gonna make no lampshade out of me."

A character, he was also apparently bad at managing his calendar. For Ellis, June 12, 1970, began in a way unlike many other summer mornings—he had the day off. As he'd recount a decade and a half later, his team, the Pittsburgh Pirates had just finished a two-game series in San Francisco and were en route to San Diego, and it was not Ellis's turn to pitch. So he spent the day prior in Los Angeles with some friends, relaxing—and dropping acid. It was not until the morning of the 12th that his friend's girlfriend told him that the Pirates had a doubleheader in San Diego that afternoon and, because of the extra game, Ellis was expected to take the mound. He hopped onto a shuttle and made it to the ballpark in time to start his game. Through the nine innings he pitched, he struck out six batters, walked eight, but gave up no hits—and won, 2–0. (Who knew LSD could be a performance-enhancing drug?)

In the book *The Harder They Fall: Celebrities Tell Their Real Life Stories of Addiction and Recovery*, Ellis recounted his LSD-addled view of the historic game:

> I can only remember bits and pieces of the game. I was psyched. I had a feeling of euphoria. I was zeroed in on the (catcher's) glove, but I didn't hit the glove too much. I remember hitting a couple of batters, and the bases were loaded two or three times. The ball was small sometimes, the ball was large sometimes, sometimes I saw the catcher, sometimes I didn't. Sometimes, I tried to stare the hitter down and throw while I was looking at him. I chewed my gum until it turned to powder. I started having a crazy idea in the fourth inning that Richard Nixon was the home plate umpire, and once I thought I was pitching a baseball to Jimi Hendrix, who to me was holding a

guitar and swinging it over the plate. They say I had about three to four fielding chances. I remember diving out of the way of a ball I thought was a line drive. I jumped, but the ball wasn't hit hard and never reached me.

Ellis retired from Major League Baseball after the 1979 season and turned over a new leaf: He became a drug addiction counselor. He passed away in December of 2008 at age sixty-three.

BONUS FACT

Major League Baseball pitcher Jim Abbott was born without a right hand. Nevertheless, he had a ten-year career in the league, and on September 4, 1993, threw a no-hitter.

PERFORMANCE ENHANCING INJURIES
CAN INJURIES MAKE YOU A BETTER ATHLETE?

In recent years, competitive sports have been marked with athletes using performance-enhancing drugs (PED) to gain advantages, Lance Armstrong, perhaps most famously. But drugs aren't the only way to get ahead. For some—paralympians, specifically—there's something called "boosting," no drugs required.

Only a broken toe here or there. On purpose.

The body handles a bunch of functions seemingly by itself, such as breathing, digesting, sweating, and regulating blood pressure and heart rate. All these things happen in a way that we can't truly control—try and get your brain to convince your body to stop sweating or speed up your heart rate and you'll almost certainly fail. This is true whether you're a paralympian or a paralegal.

But people who have suffered spinal cord injuries often find their bodies no longer appropriately regulate their blood pressure or heart rate. Because of this, when they exercise or compete in athletic competitions, their bodies do not adapt properly to increase the flow of oxygen available to the lungs and other organs. Without an increased oxygen supply, their bodies tire more quickly than a typical athlete's would. But because this affects most of them, the playing field is level.

Until they bring the pain. Literally.

People with certain spinal cord injuries may be susceptible to something called autonomic dysreflexia. Autonomic dysreflexia occurs when something below the point of the spinal injury becomes irritated, and, because of the spinal injury, the brain isn't notified about the irritation and therefore cannot act. Instead, reflex takes over, and the person's pulse increases and blood pressure rises. Usually, this is very dangerous and at times life threatening. But for these athletes, it gives a boost in the areas where they need it most.

Autonomic dysreflexia can be self-induced in various ways, such as breaking a bone (commonly a toe, as mentioned above) below the point of the spinal injury, or overfilling one's bladder via a clamped catheter. And for these athletes, the increased endurance they get from this is real—a study in the journal *Nature* stated that "the efficacy of boosting was a resulting significant decrease in race time with a mean improvement of 9.7% in race performance."

In 1994, the International Paralympic Committee (IPC) banned boosting—but because it's hard to catch, it still happens widely. In 2012, the BBC reported that the IPC conducted a survey during the 2008 Paralympic Games in Beijing, and 17 percent of athletes (anonymously) admitted to boosting at least once in their careers.

BONUS FACT

The name "Paralympics" has nothing to do with paraplegia. The prefix para- is derived from a Greek word meaning "alongside," as, since 1988 in Seoul, South Korea, the Paralympics are played in the same year and city as the main Olympic Games. (The term "paralegal" has the same etymology, meaning a person who works alongside lawyers.)

DOUBLE BONUS!

PED use in cycling has a long history—just ask the late Henri Desgrange, credited with founding the Tour de France. According to Wikipedia, when Desgrange issued the rule book for the 1930 Tour, he specifically noted that performance-enhancing drugs would not be provided by race organizers, implying that racers were to seek their own.

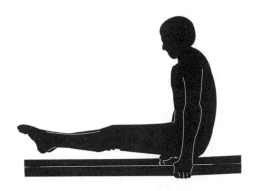

WOOD MEDALIST
THE OLYMPIAN WHO BROKE THE PROSTHETICS BARRIER

The third modern Summer Olympics took place in St. Louis, Missouri, in 1904. In total, these Olympic Games lasted months, coinciding with the World's Fair which St. Louis hosted that same year. The now-familiar men's gymnastics competition occurred primarily on October 28 of that year, well past the end of the summer. It lasted one day, with eight events plus an awards ceremony for combined excellence in the parallel bars, horizontal bar, vault, and pommel horse.

The number and nationalities of most of the competitors is unknown, lost to antiquity. All we know are the names of the medalists—all of them American—and where they placed. Two men, Anton Heida (five golds, one silver) and George Eyser (three golds, two silvers, and a bronze) took home medals in six events—not a bad day. Heida fared better than Eyser; he also had a distinct advantage over the second-best man that day. Unlike Eyser, Heida had two legs.

In 1848, a spate of revolutions spread through Europe, mostly fueled by the middle class. In Germany, one such revolution was led by a group called the Turnverein—literally, the "gymnastic unions."

These groups were comprised of mostly working-class males who, beyond gathering to learn the art of gymnastics, also found a common bond in politics. But when the revolution of 1848 failed, the gymnasiums closed and many Turnverein left Germany. Most ended up in the United States, where they became a group called the Turners.

George Eyser was born in Germany in 1870 and emigrated to the St. Louis area at age fourteen. Sometime during his adolescence, likely before his family left Germany (although much of Eyser's biography is unknown), he lost his left leg after being hit by a train. He was outfitted with a wooden prosthesis, allowing him to run, jump, and otherwise participate in many athletics. The Turners were the prevailing German-American social circle in St. Louis at the time. If you were German, gymnastics was part and parcel of the St. Louis community experience, and Eyser's lack of a left leg did not change this at all.

Eyser's experience as a gymnast paid off. Even though the competitors in the 1904 Olympics were, compared to today's athletes, rank amateurs—the Games simply did not have the draw or importance that they'd later develop—Eyser dominated. He took gold metals on the parallel bars, vault (tying with Heida), and in the long-discontinued twenty-five-foot rope climb. He also took a bronze on the horizontal bar and pommel horse, and, due to his combined success, took the "combined four events" silver.

Eyser's medals in the 1904 Games would be the last won by a person with an artificial leg until the 2012 games in London. His mere participation in the Games was also a century-long feat—not until 2008, when South African swimmer Natalie de Toit participated in the Beijing Games, did another person with an artificial leg compete in the Olympics.

BONUS FACT

If you look at the 1904 Summer Olympics results, you'll also see a men's gymnastics event that took place on July 1 and 2, with medals awarded to the top three teams, the three best all-around gymnasts, and the top three finishers in the "men's triathlon." The triathlon consisted of the horizontal bar, parallel bars, and the horse (itself split into vault and pommel horse). Eyser finished tenth. But the other two events were a mix of gymnastics and what we'd now call track and field. Those events consisted of the gymnastic triathlon as well as the "athletic triathlon"—shot put, the 100-yard dash, and the long jump. Eyser, at a distinct disadvantage in the track-and-field portions, finished seventy-first in the all-around.

OUT OF SYNC
AN OLYMPIC MEDALIST'S HIDDEN SECRET

In the 2001 World Aquatics Championship in Fukuoka, Japan, a fifteen-year-old Chinese diver, Wu Minxia, and her partner, Guo Jingjing, took gold in the women's synchronized springboard competition. For Wu, this would be the start of well over a decade of dominance. She'd earn gold in the event at the 2003, 2007, 2009, and 2011 World Aquatics Championships. Even more impressively, she took gold at the 2004 Olympics in Athens, the 2008 Games in Beijing, and the 2012 London Games—becoming the first woman diver to win gold medals at three different Olympics.

Reaching such heights requires some sacrifice, and for many Olympic-class athletes, their partners, coaches, trainers, and the like are akin to family. But in Wu's case, that's an understatement. Those people were, undoubtedly, closer to the diver than she was to her own parents. We know this because of what happened soon after Wu won her record-setting Olympic gold medal in Athens.

According to the AFP, Wu's parents had decided to hide some family news from their daughter until after her final Olympic dive. After she took the medal stand (although thankfully, not immediately after), they informed her that two of her grandparents had died—more than a year prior. Perhaps worse, they told her that her mother had breast cancer and had been battling it for eight years. (By the time of the Olympics, it was fortunately in remission.) Wu had, effectively, lived a separate life from her family.

Other reports flew in. According to TheWeek.com, Wu spent the ten years prior to the London Games separated from her parents. At age sixteen—just a few months after her gold in Fukuoka—she left home to attend a government-run swimming and diving school. Her parents told the media that they've "known for years that [their] daughter doesn't belong to [them] any more," and admitted that they "never talk about family matters" with her.

Even that may be an understatement. As the AFP reported, when Wu's parents arrived in London for the 2012 games, they barely communicated with her before the diving event—they sent her a text message, telling her they had arrived safely, but otherwise had no contact with their daughter.

They did not even go see her before her final dive.

The Chinese rank and file did not take kindly to these admissions. Many took to the microblogging service Sina Weibo (similar to Twitter, but censored and controlled by the Chinese government), bemoaning the parents' actions. But their ire wasn't focused only on the Wu family. Many blamed the national sports program—which, as Yahoo! reported, took a very hardline view toward earning victory: That year, the government sent official congratulations to gold medalists, but not to those earning silver or bronze.

Unfortunately, that is unlikely to change. The London Games were the third consecutive Olympics in which China finished in the top two on the medal count table (in this case, behind the United States), and the government likely sees the disintegration of the athletes' families' lives as an acceptable cost.

BONUS FACT

In March of 2012, China sacked high-level politician Bo Xilai, causing a rift in the Chinese Politburo. On one side was Bo's ally, Zhou Yong-kang, who, per the rumor mill, was aiming at pulling off a coup. On the other side was the premier, Wen Jiabao, one of Bo's chief rivals. Sina Weibo users quickly found themselves unable to use these names, as the censors stepped in, hoping to stop conversations around the topic of internal political strife. To compensate, the online world invented nicknames for many of the players, borrowing terms from popular culture which, according to the AFP, "share[d] a common character in Chinese" with the banned names. Zhou became "Mister Kong," a brand of noodle, and Wen became "Teletubbies."

TO KILL A SPARROW
THE UNINTENDED CONSEQUENCES OF KILLING BIRDS

Mao Zedong controlled China with an iron fist for more than three decades and is widely believed to have caused the death of roughly 50 million people during his reign. His two main political campaigns—the Great Leap Forward and the Cultural Revolution—are considered terrible failures in large part because of the death toll and suppression of human rights. One of the reasons for the massive death toll? A fickle, half-baked idea of Mao's called the Four Pests Campaign.

In 1958, Mao decided that the health and hygiene of the average Chinese citizen were of vital importance. As one his first acts as part of the Great Leap Forward, he took aim at four creatures—the "Four Pests"—that the supreme ruler believed were putting his people at risk of disease. Mao figured that if he could eliminate these creatures, he would thereby create massive health gains throughout his nation.

Of the four pests, three of them—mosquitoes, flies, and rats—may have made sense to single out among the animal kingdom. But rendering them extinct, even locally, is a fool's errand. Mao was willing to play the fool, as evidenced by the fourth creature on his list—the sparrow. Chairman Mao observed that sparrows ate the grains planted by Chinese workers, at times ransacking fields, and, therefore, the birds were responsible for reducing the value of the people's labor. Sparrows were added to the hit list and given priority—they were more effectively targeted than the other three "pests." Mao's government began a large-scale propaganda campaign to get peasants to shoo or kill sparrows on sight. People of all ages were encouraged to engage in this War Against Sparrows. Posters from the campaign still exist, with one particular one showing a child armed with a slingshot with the message "Everyone come and fight sparrows."

The propaganda worked. The Four Pests Campaign was incredibly successful, as the sparrow was nearly rendered extinct in China.

Unfortunately, the Four Pests Campaign was also a wonderful example of the Law of Unintended Consequences. The sparrows did not just eat grains. They also ate insects—specifically, locusts. Locusts, like sparrows, also ate grains, and now, without a natural predator to keep their population in check, the insects thrived beyond expectation. The swarms of locusts ate a lot more grain than the sparrows ever could.

By the time Mao's government noticed and could react, two years had passed, and the damage was already done. The ecological imbalance caused by the Four Pests Campaign helped spur on massive food shortages and, in turn, the deaths of hundreds of thousands, if not millions, of people.

BONUS FACT

What one society considers a pest may be considered a boon by another. In Uganda, for example, fried grasshoppers are a delicacy, served with onions (and with their wings removed). Grasshopper collectors use bright lights to attract large numbers of the insects to gather in a small area, and then quickly gas and capture them. Unfortunately, the method of attracting the bugs doesn't always work in the underdeveloped nation. In December 2011, Uganda was struck with a large number of power outages—meaning no lights, and therefore, a grasshopper shortage.

THE COBRA EFFECT
HOW A MANDATE FOR DEATH CAN BREED NEW LIFE

If you want to get something done, it probably makes sense to ask people to provide the service, and, in most cases, pay them for doing so. Give a proper incentive and people will rise to the call of duty—or, at least, that's what we hope will happen. Sometimes, though, things go wrong because the incentive accidentally makes the problem worse. Enter the Cobra Effect.

Vikas Mehrotra is a professor of finance at the University of Alberta. In 2012, he joined Stephen Dubner and Steven Levitt, authors of the best-selling book *Freakonomics*, on their podcast. He recounted an incident from India, back when it was still under control of the British crown. At the time, according to Mehrotra's anecdote, Delhi had a problem—lots of venomous cobras were roaming the streets, putting the lives of people at risk. The government's solution? Kill all the cobras.

To accomplish this goal, the government employed a pretty straightforward strategy—institute a bounty. If a person killed a cobra, the government would reward him or her with some money. The more cobras you killed, the more money you got, so people sharpened their knives and broke out their clubs.

The problem? Catching and killing a wild cobra is hard, as it should be, in order to justify the bounty system in the first place. But capturing a few cobras and starting your own breed of the snakes is not much harder—and then, you're left with a perpetually self-replenishing supply of cobras that you don't have to chase down. An enterprising would-be cobra killer can simply grow his own cobra clan, kill some, collect the reward, rinse, repeat.

When news of the scheme hit the government, as Mehrotra's story goes, they did the only thing they could and ended the bounty program. Unfortunately, the cobra farmers now had piles of venomous, worthless cobras and no incentive to kill them (and risk being bitten). So they didn't. Instead, the cobra farmers released their hordes of contraband creatures into the streets, redoubling the problem.

Today, the term "Cobra Effect" is used to describe such an unintended outcome of an otherwise straightforward plan.

BONUS FACT

Mehotra's story may be apocryphal, but we know that the Cobra Effect is real. Michael Vann, a professor of history at Sacramento State University, published a paper in 2003 titled "Of Rats, Rice, and Race: The Great Hanoi Rat Massacre" in the academic journal *French Colonial History*. In the late 1800s, France controlled Vietnam and built out Hanoi's sewer system—a by-product of which was the explosion of the rat population. When the problem became too large for exterminators to handle, the French administrators of the city offered a bounty for catching and killing the rats, with payment to be made upon the presentation of the rats' tails. The bounties ended when authorities realized that a new cottage industry had developed just outside the city limits—rat farming, designed for the easy harvest of rat tails.

THE APTLY NAMED SNAKE ISLAND
WHERE DEATH IS JUST A FEW METERS AWAY

On the coast of Sao Paolo, Brazil sits Ilha de Queimada Grande, or as it is known colloquially in English, Snake Island. The island, roughly 110 acres of trees, is uninhabited, with only one building—a lighthouse—abandoned for years. Despite the tropical nature of the Queimada Grande, travel to the island is expressly forbidden by the Brazilian navy. Why? Because Queimada Grande is home to hundreds of thousands of golden lanceheads, a snake you probably don't want to get too close to.

Golden lanceheads are unique to Queimada Grande. The snake typically grows to be about two feet long but can at extremes grow to nearly double that length. And it is venomous—very, very venomous.

Generally lanceheads (that is, the more common cousins of the golden lancehead) are responsible for 90 percent of snake bite-related fatalities in Brazil. The mortality rate from a lancehead bite is 7 percent if the wound goes untreated, and even treatment doesn't guarantee survival. Roughly 3 percent of those who are bitten by lanceheads and treated with antivenom still end up dying from the bite. The venom causes a grab bag of symptoms, including kidney failure, necrosis of muscular tissue, brain hemorrhaging, and intestinal bleeding. Scary stuff, to be sure.

No official records tell of a person being bitten by a snake, let alone a golden lancehead-caused fatality, because the *de facto* quarantine on the island has successfully kept humans separated from these deadly beasts. In fact, there is reason to believe that snakes of the golden variety are much more dangerous than their continental cousins. A chemical analysis of golden lancehead venom suggests that it is faster acting and more powerful—perhaps five times more powerful. Surviving a golden lancehead attack, especially when on an otherwise isolated island, is a tall order.

The only way to guarantee survival is to avoid these two-foot-long monsters altogether, which is primarily why Snake Island is closed to tourists—encountering a golden lancehead there is an all-but-certain fate. Even the most conservative estimate suggests that the golden lancehead population density on Queimada Grande is one per square meter; others suggest the population is as high as *five* per square meter. Regardless, as Atlas Obscura points out, even at the lower estimate, "you're never more than three feet away from death."

BONUS FACT

Another reason to keep Snake Island free from visitors is to protect the snakes themselves. The International Union for Conservation of Nature, or IUCN, is an international organization that publishes the "Red List of Threatened Species," the leading taxonomy of species that are at risk of extinction. The Red List has three levels in the "threatened" risk category, with "vulnerable" being the lowest risk category therein, followed by "endangered," and finally, "critically endangered." The golden lancehead is considered "critically endangered" by the IUCN because the snake meets two key criteria: It only exists at a single location of less than 100 kilometers-squared (Snake Island) and that habitat is in decline, due to human interference. For a while, Brazil wanted to slash-and-burn the terrain and turn it into a banana planta-tion. Those plans never came to fruition, and since 2004, the golden lancehead population has been stable.

WHERE THE BODIES GO
WHAT HAPPENS WHEN A HOMELESS NEW YORKER DIES?

Roughly 7 million people live in New York City, and, like everywhere else in the world, some of them die. Sometimes, they die with no family and/or no money. In New York, a few thousand such people die each year in the city's hospitals alone. But these people's stories do not end with their deaths. What does the city do with the bodies?

The answer? They're buried on Hart Island.

Hart Island is located in the western part of Long Island Sound, a few miles offshore from the Bronx and only a bit farther from Queens. This tiny island—131 acres—has been uninhabited for years, at least by the living. Since 1869, the city of New York has used the island as a potter's field, a burial ground for those who could not afford burial elsewhere. The potter's field now takes up roughly 101 of the island's 131 acres and is the largest tax-supported graveyard in the world.

More than 850,000 people have been buried on Hart's Island, and roughly 2,000 more burials occur each year. Dismembered body parts constitute a small minority of the burials. An estimated one-third of the burials are of very young children. With one exception—"special child baby 1 1985," the first child to die of AIDS in New York City—the bodies are buried in mass graves. Children are buried in trenches numbering as many as 1,000 each, whereas adults—whose bodies are often disinterred when relatives later claim them—are buried in three sections of roughly fifty each.

What to see if you know anyone buried there? To find out, you need to peruse the records, which are maintained by the city's Department of Correction—a strange quirk of how the island is administered. Because of the cost of burying 2,000 or so bodies (or parts thereof) each year, the city uses prison labor for the job. Inmates from Rikers Island, New York City's jail, are ferried over to Hart's Island and paid 50 cents per hour to stack coffins for burial. Since the 1950s, the burials occur without any sort of ceremony; grave sites are not even outfitted with markers indicating those buried.

The city, generally, does not allow visitors, press, or tourists to see some still-present historical landmarks on the island, citing security concerns due to the fact that prisoners work there. The only exceptions made are to family members of the deceased who may be buried there, and even in that case, the visits must be scheduled with the Department of Correction and the visitors are not allowed to visit the gravesites unaccompanied.

BONUS FACT

Legend has it that Hart Island is haunted. This isn't the case, of course. But if you were a homeowner on Hart Island (again, not the case, as it is uninhabited) and told tales about such ghosts, you couldn't sell your home without disclosing that to a would-be buyer. In 1991, the New York court system decided the case of *Stambovsky vs. Ackley*, holding that if a seller promoted (in that case, via years of stories to the local press) his or her home as being haunted, the courts would hold him or her to that belief. As a poltergeist in one's home is a material defect of the house (assuming you aren't a Ghostbuster) that cannot be detected by any nonparanormal method of inspection, the court held that the seller must inform the purchaser of the presence of the ghosts. Failure to do so, as seller Ackley did in the above-mentioned case, entitles the buyer to his or her deposit back.

SLAYING THE SILVER BALL
PROOF THAT ALMOST ANYTHING CAN BE BANNED

Fiorello LaGuardia was elected mayor of New York City in 1933, and, on January 1 of the following year, took office. One of his first acts as mayor was to crack down on mafia activity, especially mob-owned slot machines, seeing them as a direct line into the coffers of organized crime. LaGuardia paid personal attention to the confiscation and destruction of the machines, taking a sledgehammer along with the media in tow to snap pictures.

But with this one income source down, the mafia was not about to give up on gambling altogether. As *Mental Floss* magazine noted, the mobsters turned to something else: pinball machines. LaGuardia's ire refocused on pinball as well.

LaGuardia was already anything but fond of pinball; according to *Popular Mechanics*, he stated in an affidavit submitted to the Supreme Court that pinball hit the "pockets of schoolchildren in the form of nickels and dimes given them as lunch money." And he was probably correct. Pinball operators were known to allow players to exchange the replays and extra balls they earned for cash. This effectively turned the machines into complicated slot machines, especially in cases where these bonuses were awarded randomly, and not due to player skill. Over time, he succeeded in getting the game declared an illegal game of chance, and in 1940, New York City banned pinball within its borders.

Like most contraband, this simply pushed pinball underground, into seedy parlors and strip joints in Greenwich Village and Harlem. Popular disdain for pinball did not approach that for slot machines, making it hard for LaGuardia to muster up support for raids on illegal pinball establishments—until December 1941. That year, the Japanese attacked Pearl Harbor, thrusting the United States into World War II. In January 1942, the Federal government established the "Salvage for Victory" campaign, calling on Americans to turn in scrap metal to be used in the war effort. As reported by *The New York Times*, LaGuardia and team went on a hunt for pinball machines to further these efforts. By February, they confiscated (and again, sledgehammered) more than 3,000 machines, turning roughly 2,500 of them into one ton of metal for the war. The pinball ban in New York lasted for decades, outliving LaGuardia (who died in 1947).

Music may have been the driving force behind the reintroduction of pinball into New York and other cities. In 1969, The Who released the album *Tommy*, which told the story of a "deaf, dumb and blind kid" who became a superstar pinball player despite his apparent disabilities. The album hit number four on the *Billboard* pop charts and the song "Pinball Wizard" peaked at number nineteen on the U.S. *Billboard* charts that year. In 1975, *Tommy* was adapted as a film, further reinvigorating demand and interest in pinball.

In 1976, New York City reinstated pinball—but perhaps only due to a stroke of luck. Roger Sharpe, a magazine editor in his mid-twenties, testified in front of the city council that pinball was a game of skill, not luck, and therefore shouldn't be regulated as a game of chance. The city council required more convincing. So Sharpe took to the machine, pulled back the plunger, and told the council members that he'd skillfully drop the ball into the middle slot, in what he'd later admit was a bluff. The ball went exactly where he said it would, and the council voted to allow pinball back into the city.

BONUS FACT

Another thing LaGuardia banned in the name of fighting the mob? Artichoke sales. In December 1935, LaGuardia announced what, according to *The New York Times*, he called a "serious and threatening emergency": The price of artichokes had greatly inflated due to price fixing by the mafia. LaGuardia barred the sale, display, and even possession of artichokes. Amazingly, this worked. When prices came down a year later, LaGuardia rescinded the order.

THE FREE CITY OF TRI-INSULA
NEW YORK CITY CONSIDERS A SOLO CAREER

The 2002 movie *Gangs of New York* takes place in the mid-1800s, during a period when New York City was divided over the possibilities of a civil war. Although the movie itself is fiction, many of the plot points are drawn from history. For example, in July 1863, many working-class New Yorkers rioted over the Union's decision to institute a military draft. During the four-day clash between rioters and federal troops, more than 100 people were killed and another 2,000 were wounded. The riot was, eventually, suppressed.

This wasn't the first time New York City's skepticism toward the sanctity of the United States came into play. In early 1861, the city considered leaving the country and becoming its own nation.

In December 1860, South Carolina seceded from the Union, sparking troop mobilizations and dividing the populace. Although northern states such as New York (and by extension, New York City) were, by and large, antislavery and pro-Union, this was hardly unanimous. Feeling of unity with the South and disdain for the Union was, probably, a minority opinion, but those sympathetic to the rebels had an ally in high places: the mayor's office.

Mayor Fernando Wood, who served as the city's chief executive for two nonconsecutive terms, was what was known as a Copperhead—a Northern Democrat who was in favor of a peaceful resolution with the Southern states, in most cases even if it meant a continuation of slavery. In 1861—a few months before the Civil War began—Wood believed that the Union was destined to crumble and, in any event, saw the national government as no friend to his city. Much of New York's mercantile industry's business—one of the largest industries in the city at the time—came from the cotton trade. Tariffs imposed by the federal government—plus the likelihood of trade disruptions due to secessions, if not war—put that at risk. (Wood was no abolitionist either—he had a reputation for racism and for facilitating slavery, legal and illegal alike.)

On January 6, 1861, Wood proposed that the city leave New York State, and therefore the Union. Wood's plan was for Staten Island and Long Island (including Brooklyn and Queens, which at the time were not part of New York City) to form an independent city-state called the Free City of Tri-Insula. When he proposed it, the city council's reaction was lukewarm at best, although hardly unanimously against declaring independence. Before Wood could drum up support for his plan, Confederate troops fired on Fort Sumter, and by and large, the city's leadership rallied around Abraham Lincoln. Wood failed to win re-election in 1862. His successor, George Opdyke, was an antislavery Republican whose most notable act as mayor was recruiting troops to quell the anti-draft riots of 1863.

BONUS FACT

When was the last time a politician proposed that New York City secede from the state? That occurred in 2008, when a city councilman,

Peter Vallone Jr., from Queens, offered a bill that, if passed, would (purportedly) lead to New York City becoming the fifty-first state. Earlier that week, Michael Bloomberg, the city's mayor, testified that New York City paid out $11 billion more in taxes to the state than it received in services. Seceding, Vallone argued, was the only solution. The bill went nowhere. To date, New York City is still part of New York State.

THE NORTH IN THE SOUTH
THE CIVIL WAR'S TINY CIVIL WAR

In January of 1861, representatives from across Alabama gathered at a convention to decide whether to adopt an ordinance of secession, the formal document by which the state attempted to secede from the Union. (Each of the other seceding states issued their own such documents in various different ways.) The convention, by a sixty-one yea, thirty-nine nay vote, decided to secede and become part of the Confederate States of America, and almost all the delegates signed the ordinance once the majority established its passage. One exception to this was Charles Christopher Sheats, a twenty-one-year-old schoolteacher, and the lone delegate from Winston County.

Although Sheats's decision made him an outcast if not an outright enemy of Alabama and the Confederacy as a whole, he accurately portrayed the desires of his home in Winston County. Winston, covering a generally hilly region unsuitable for typical plantation-style farms, had a relatively small population and even smaller population of slaves; per the 1860 census, fewer than 3,500 white people and 122 slaves lived there. (For comparison's sake, the state as a whole had a population of about 520,000 free people and

435,000 slaves.) With an end to slavery being an important, if not the only, driving force behind the South's collective decision to leave the Union, the Winston population feared that plantation owners were looking to expand their power, which would certainly come at the expense of nonplantation areas of Alabama such as their own.

Over time, Winston's dissent from secession became increasingly tangible. As the Civil War continued, Winston's government took a neutral stance, refusing to support either side. Citizens of the county did not enlist in the Confederate ranks and refused to take loyalty oaths pledging themselves to the Confederacy. And as Confederate actions in the area (such as attempts at forced conscription) increased, Winston's citizenry became less and less receptive to the South's cause, turning pro-Union. Sheats himself was jailed by Confederates for his support of the North, and at one point the county considered a resolution to, themselves, secede from Alabama—if the state could secede from the Union, they argued, the county could secede from the state. News of the resolution spread throughout the region, leading many to believe that Winston had declared itself an independent nation, separate from both North and South.

But the resolution never passed, in large part because of the still-significant number of pro-Confederate people in the county. The county became a microcosm of the country, with people on both sides seizing arms, destroying property, and taking each other's lives. Some Winston men enlisted with the Union army when the North invaded Alabama in 1862, joining the 1st Alabama Cavalry Regiment, which later accompanied William Tecumseh Sherman in his famous march to the sea. Others joined up the Confederate Home Guard, a militia designed to track down deserters and act as last defense against a Union invasion. Those Unionists who did not join the cavalry created their own version of the home guard, adding to the violence in the region.

Today, Winston is best known as the county that seceded from the Confederacy (even though it did not), and is often referred to as "the Republic of Winston" or "the Free State of Winston," even by the county's residents. The myth has spread so widely that multiple novels make reference to it, including *Addie Pray* (upon which the movie *Paper Moon* is based) and *To Kill a Mockingbird*. To mark the town's uniquely divided culture during the war, the war memorial is a statue of a young soldier, clad half in Union grays and half in Confederate garb.

BONUS FACT

In 1937, an Alabama realty company sued the city of Birmingham, claiming that the city's new parking meters—which were placed on parking spots next to the company's property—were unconstitutional. The company argued that the parking meters (and, more to the point, the requirement that one pay to park) inhibited their right to access their property and therefore was akin to a seizure of that property without due process. The Alabama Supreme Court, amazingly, agreed.

WHERE THE BAGS GO
WHAT HAPPENS TO LOST LUGGAGE?

Air travel comes with a risk that, although mathematically rare, seems all too common: lost luggage. According to *Conde Nast Traveler*, U.S. carriers handle 400 million checked bags a year, and as many as 2 million bags are lost each year from domestic U.S. flights alone. That's a small percentage—about half a percent—and most misplaced bags are reunited with their owners within forty-eight hours. Within five days, 95 percent of those 2 million bags will find themselves back home. But a small percentage—and we're talking 50,000 to 100,000—sit idly, never to find their way back home.

What happens to these bags? They go to Alabama.

Scottsboro, Alabama, is a small city of just under 15,000 people, tucked away in the northeast corner of the state, thirty miles or so from the Georgia and Tennessee borders. Every year, about a million visitors come to this tiny city, the vast majority of whom come to visit the Unclaimed Baggage Center. This 50,000-square-foot store sells the things that flyers lost and were unable to recover.

When an airline loses your bags, federal law requires them to try to find them for you. Typically, the airlines are successful at doing so. But not always. After the lost bag has sat for ninety days unclaimed (or its owner has not been located), federal law imposes a different obligation on the airlines: They have to pay the flyer a settlement amount. In doing so, the airline effectively purchases the luggage, becoming the legal owner of everything inside the bags. But airlines aren't in the business of selling random items like half-used bottles of sunscreen, underwear of every size, evening gowns, jewelry, and a cornucopia of other goods. Besides, it would be bad for business if the airlines—after scanning baggage and at times, manually inspecting the contents—started putting the high-priced items you formerly owned on some e-commerce site. (Imagine the conspiracy theories!) This leaves the airlines with a problem: Tens of thousands of bags become theirs each year, and they can't sell the stuff inside.

The Unclaimed Baggage Center is the largest and most well known of a handful of intermediaries that help solve this problem. The UBC, as Scottsboro locals call it, buys unclaimed baggage by the pound, sight unseen, from the airlines. (This works well for the airlines because they're better off having no knowledge of the contents of the unclaimed bags.) The UBC trucks the items from various airlines' unclaimed baggage depots across the country to the Scottsboro HQ. Workers sort through the contents, and about a third of the items make it onto the shelves in the colossal store. Another third are donated to charity, and the final third is deemed unfit for sale. (The criteria for being unfit for sale is unknown, but shoppers have noted that partially consumed bottles of lotion are often on the store shelves whereas sex toys rarely, if ever, are.) Most items are for sale at a sizeable discount, and on occasion, a shopper may find a diamond in the rough—literally. The UBC has sold a handful of lost diamond jewelry in its forty-plus-year history.

BONUS FACT

Sometimes, albeit rarely, airlines are better off losing luggage. This was certainly the case regarding a regional flight servicing areas of the Democratic Republic of Congo on August 25, 2010. That day, the contents of one passenger's carry-on bag resulted in tragedy. According to *NBC News*, a passenger had snuck a crocodile into a large duffle bag, hoping to sell it at his intended destination. The crocodile got loose, scared the you-know-what out of the flight crew and passengers, and caused the pilot to lose control of the plane. The plane crashed into a house (the residents were thankfully not at home), killing all but one of the twenty-one people onboard. The crocodile survived but was killed by a machete-wielding Congolese shortly thereafter.

FINDING THE *TITANIC*
HOW THE MILITARY HELPED FIND THE WORLD'S MOST FAMOUS SHIPWRECK

The RMS *Titanic* set sail from Southampton on its way to New York City on April 10, 1912. As we all know, it did not reach its destination. On April 14, the ship struck an iceberg and within hours snapped in two and sank to the Atlantic floor. The wreckage was lost at sea until September 1, 1985, when underwater archeologist Robert Ballard discovered the ship's boiler and hull while aboard the *Knorr*, a research vessel owned by the U.S. Navy.

But the *Knorr* was not out there searching for the *Titanic*. It was on a secret Cold War mission at the behest of the Navy itself.

In the early 1980s, Dr. Ballard created Argo, an unmanned undersea video camera outfitted with various lighting designed to illuminate the ocean at depths approaching 20,000 feet. The site of the *Titanic* disaster, in the seabed roughly 370 miles south-southeast of Newfoundland, put the wreckage at about 12,500 feet, well within Argo's range. But getting the camera—which out of the water weighed 4,000 pounds—to the site required a ship, crew, and a sizeable budget.

In 1982, Ballard asked the Navy to request funding for his search for the *Titanic*, but the Navy wasn't interested. It was, however, interested in Argo more generally. In the 1960s, a pair of nuclear submarines—the USS *Thresher* and USS *Scorpion*—sank. The Navy didn't know what caused the disasters, and was particularly concerned about the *Scorpion's* fate—it may have been sunk by the Soviets. Further, the military wanted to know what happened to the nuclear reactors on those ships and the impact they had on the ocean environment. So the Navy struck a deal with Ballard: help answer these questions and, if time and budget permit, you can search for the *Titanic* while you're out there, too.

Ballard managed to find both the *Thresher* and *Scorpion* with time to spare. (The *Thresher* sank due to a piping error, he concluded, according to *National Geographic*; he couldn't determine if the *Scorpion* fell prey to an attack. Neither nuclear reactor had an adverse effect on the ecology of the ocean.) With the Navy's blessing, he went toward where he believed the *Titanic* came to rest, and, correctly speculating that the ship had broken into two parts, was able to discover its location. Fanfare and major press attention ensued.

The Navy, for its part, began to worry. With the public eye now focused on Ballard's expedition, the Navy feared that his initial reason for being at sea would come to light. But apparently, no one thought to ask. Ballard's secret mission did not become public until after the fall of the Soviet Union.

BONUS FACT

The *Titanic* had two sister ships—ships of virtually the same design—called the HMHS *Britannic* and the RMS *Olympic*. Both had disasters of their own. In 1911, while under the command of Captain Edward Smith (the captain of the *Titanic* when it sunk), the *Olympic* crashed into a British warship and nearly capsized. No one died, as the ship successfully returned to shore despite two chambers taking on water.

In 1916, the *Britannic* met a fate similar to the *Titanic*'s four years prior, sinking in the Mediterranean Sea. But unlike in the *Titanic*'s accident, the vast majority—1,036 of the 1,066 people on board—survived. One of the survivors was a nurse named Violet Jessop, who also was on the *Titanic* when it sank. She is the only person to have survived both, and was also on the *Olympic* during its aforementioned collision.

THE TWO SOVIETS WHO SAVED THE WORLD
MUTUALLY ASSURED DESTRUCTION, TWICE AVOIDED

In 1961, the United States undertook a series of unsuccessful campaigns in Cuba, attempting to overthrow Fidel Castro and his regime. These campaigns—including the Bay of Pigs invasion—ultimately failed. The Soviet Union, Cuba's staunch ally at the time, reacted by working with Castro to build a secret nuclear weapons site on the island. Cuba is a stone's throw away from the continental United States, and had the weapons base been completed, any nuclear missiles there would have been able to hit American soil.

On October 12, 1962, a U.S. recon plane captured images of the base being built, sending the White House (and the American people) into panic. The United States imposed a military quarantine on Cuba, denying the Soviets the ability to bring in any weapons, and insisted that the base be dismantled. The Soviets publicly balked, and anyone alive at the time (and old enough to remember) needs no refresher: The world was on the brink of nuclear war. Roughly two weeks later, on October 28, 1962, the two nations came to an agreement, staving off what could have been a tragic result.

However, if it weren't for a Soviet naval officer named Vasili Arkhipov, there is a good chance none of us would be here today.

The day before the Americans and Soviets found a middle ground, Arkhipov was aboard a submarine patrolling the waters near Cuba. American naval forces surrounded the submarine and began dropping depth charges—a tactic the U.S. Navy used to get submarines to surface, not one intended to destroy the (assumed to be) enemy submarine.

Unfortunately, the submarine's captain either forgot about this tactic or was unaware of it, and—underwater, unable to contract Moscow—believed war had broken out. Soviet protocol at the time allowed for the use of nuclear torpedoes if the three highest-ranking sailors on the ship believed it proper. The captain and a third officer concluded it was. Arkhipov, the second in command, objected—and, thankfully, prevailed. The ship surfaced without starting World War III.

More than twenty years later, nuclear war was barely averted once again. By the early 1980s, the Soviets had developed an early warning system that aimed to detect an incoming nuclear missile attack. The system allowed the Soviets to, if need be, respond with a retaliatory missile attack. Without such a system, the incoming missiles would likely destroy or disable the Soviet arsenal before it could be deployed. The protocol was simple: If the monitoring station discovered missiles headed for the Soviet Union, the leadership there was to notify its superiors. The powers that be would then decide whether the U.S.S.R. should launch its own strike, and, given the tensions at the time, it is likely they would have.

On September 26, 1983, the monitoring station detected an incoming missile. Then, it detected four more. Stanislav Petrov, the lieutenant colonel and ranking officer on site, did something incredible: He unilaterally decided that the monitoring equipment had erred, and he declined to report the "attack" to the Kremlin. Petrov based this belief on a few key factors. First, the equipment was very new and believed to be a bit buggy (although not to this degree); and second, Petrov believed that a U.S. strike would involve hundreds of warheads, not five.

Petrov turned out to be correct. The satellites were not functioning properly and the "missiles" were phantoms. Ground-based systems, a few minutes after the satellites erred, saw nothing, corroborating Petrov's belief. But Petrov did not view himself a hero. Later in life, he said that he was just doing his job and, in fact (quite literally), he did nothing at all.

BONUS FACT

During a sound check prior to giving a radio address in 1984, then-President Ronald Reagan jokingly said into the microphone, "My fellow Americans, I'm pleased to tell you today that I've signed legislation that will outlaw Russia forever. We begin bombing in five minutes." Contrary to popular belief, that audio was not actually broadcast over the airwaves. It was, however, recorded and later leaked to the press.

BLAME CUBA
HOW AMERICA'S NEIGHBOR TO THE SOUTH ALMOST BECAME A MAJOR SCAPEGOAT

In April 1961, roughly 1,500 American-trained Cuban exiles invaded their homeland in an attempt to overthrow Fidel Castro's government. That assault, now referred to as the Bay of Pigs invasion, ended in failure. The Cuban militia overwhelmed the attackers, capturing 80 percent of them and killing most of the other 20 percent. The political fallout in the United States was massive, and the desire of Americans to further engage Cuba in battle was understandably low. Further, other nations questioned America's attack on a neighboring sovereign, especially one that had shown little in the way of aggression toward the United States and was already the subject of American economic sanctions.

But the Cold War was in full force. The United States saw Cuba as a surrogate for the Soviet Union and having a Soviet stronghold just ninety miles off Florida troubled the leadership of the American military. The Department of Defense (DOD) and the military's Joint Chiefs of Staff (JCS) felt the need to revive civilian interest in overthrowing Castro and liberating Cuba. Absent a Cuban strike on Americans, though, this seemed unlikely, and no such Cuban strike appeared imminent.

So the DOD and JCS proposed to create such an attack themselves. A fake one, aimed at turning public opinion against Castro and in favor of continued military action against Cuba.

The plan, devised in 1962 and code named Operation Northwoods, had a simple yet striking goal: "to place the United States in the apparent position of suffering defensible grievances from a rash and irresponsible government of Cuba and to develop an international image of a Cuban threat to peace in the Western Hemisphere." The details, outlined in an appendix to an originally classified document titled "Pretexts to Justify U.S. Military Intervention in Cuba," included:

- Using friendly Cubans, pretending to be enemy fighters, to stage a fake (as in, there'd be no actual firearms discharge) attack on the U.S. base in Guantanamo Bay, Cuba, complete with mock funerals after. This plan may have included blowing up grounded planes and/or igniting ammunition stores on base to suggest sabotage—and of course, the fake saboteurs would be "captured."
- Blowing up a U.S. ship (again, unoccupied) somewhere near or within Cuban waters, and blaming the assault on Cuba's air force or naval batteries.
- Creating a group of fake Cuban terrorist cells, targeting Cuban refugees in the United States. The plan allowed for some bodily harm to come to the targets—"to the extent of wounding"—and also called for "sink[ing] a boatload of Cubans en route to Florida (real or simulated)."
- Painting U.S. fighter jets to look like Soviet MIGs and then harassing civilian flights with these planes—potentially looping in the commercial pilots to help convince passengers of the ruse.
- Potentially shooting down an aircraft traveling from the United States to Central America, purportedly transporting

college students (but actually empty), as it passed over Cuban air space.

In almost all cases, the plan was designed to avoid killing American civilians, although the same could not be said for "boatload[s] of Cubans" destined for Miami. Regardless, the total death toll from Operation Northwoods was zero. Then-President John F. Kennedy rejected the idea and removed its lead proponent, General Lyman Lemnitzer, from his position as the Chairman of the Joint Chiefs of Staff.

BONUS FACT

The U.S. embargo of Cuba dates back to 1960 and its reach has been adjusted a few times since. (In general, the restrictions have been tightened, but on July 16, 2012, a U.S.-sanctioned ship carrying humanitarian goods from Cubans in Miami to their families sailed into Havana, showing a recent loosening of the rules.) The ban on importing Cuban cigars was not among the original restrictions—that was added in an executive order signed by President Kennedy in 1962. But JFK was, apparently, fond of the cigars. According to Pierre Salinger, then the President's press secretary, one evening that year JFK asked him to pick up about 1,000 cigars by "tomorrow morning." Salinger over-delivered, obtaining 1,200, and presented them to the President the next morning. As Salinger recounts: "Kennedy smiled, and opened up his desk. He took out a long paper, which he immediately signed. It was the decree banning all Cuban products from the United States. Cuban cigars were now illegal in our country."

INVADING CANADA
THE U.S. PLAN TO INVADE ITS NORTHERN NEIGHBOR

The United States and Canada, by and large, have been peaceful neighbors—especially since Canada became a *de facto* independent nation under the British North America Act in 1867. But although the two nations are friendly and, typically, allies, things can change. And in 1927, the United States planned for just a scenario.

At the time, Canada was still mostly under British control, and even though the United States and the United Kingdom were friendly—they fought on the same side in the Great War—things could change quickly. The United States was concerned that the UK's imperial desires, albeit unlikely, could extend back to the United States and America was not going to be caught unprepared. The U.S. Army, therefore, developed "War Plan Red," a comprehensive strategy to foil any British expansion into its former colony.

War Plan Red assumed that in the case of war, Britain had two significant advantages. First, the British navy was a formidable force, able to control the seaways and therefore the U.S. export economy. Second, the UK controlled Canada and could use it as a staging ground for an invasion of the United States. The American plan was to strike Canada first.

Specifically, U.S. forces would invade Nova Scotia, hoping to take Halifax, which (American strategists assumed) would be the focal point for the British navy in North America. If this failed, the U.S. would try to take New Brunswick, isolating Nova Scotia from the mainland. After securing that region, American forces would target Quebec City, further separating east from west; Ontario, taking control of much of Canada's manufacturing (at the time); Winnipeg, a railway transit hub; and Vancouver, as a way of controlling the Pacific ports. War Plan Red only laid plans for military action in the Western Hemisphere—America never intended to attack the British Isles. Rather, the plan was to hold Canada hostage, so to speak, in hopes that Britain would agree to a peace treaty to free its largest New World territory. Although the plan never came into play, it probably would have worked. The UK never had a plan to attack the United States, and was willing to let the U.S. overtake Canada if push came to shove—so long as the United States did not blockade the British Isles.

In 1974, the United States declassified War Plan Red, which created a temporary ripple in U.S./Canadian relations—but it quickly passed.

BONUS FACT

The United States was not the only North American country with intracontinental war plans. In 1921—six years before War Plan Red was drafted—Canada developed its own plan, named Defence Scheme No. 1. The scheme outlined plans for a counterattack on the United States in case of an invasion from its neighbor to the south. Like War Plan Red, the plan was never put into action. Unlike War Plan Red, Scheme No. 1 was short lived—it was terminated in 1928 in an effort to foster a stronger relationship between the United States and Britain.

THE PIG WAR
WHY THE U.S. AND CANADA ALMOST
WENT TO WAR OVER LIVESTOCK

The United States and Britain have been adversaries at war, offi-cially, twice: the American Revolution and the War of 1812. In more modern times, the two nations have been allies. But for a few months in 1859, the two sides were again hostile, meeting each other in the field of battle, with over 400 American sol-diers (and roughly a dozen cannons) facing off against more than 2,000 British troops—and five British warships.

The good news: the total casualty count from the war was one—one pig, that is.

After the War of 1812, most of the Pacific Northwest was jointly occupied by both the United States and the United King-dom. Over time, the two nations came to an agreement—the Oregon Treaty—that divided the territory at the 49th Parallel, forming the modern border between the state of Washington (U.S.) and the province of British Columbia (Canada). An excep-tion was made for Vancouver Island, which was placed entirely under British control even though it dipped below the 49th Par-allel. The Oregon Treaty specifically drew the line of demarcation separating the two at "the middle of the channel which separates the continent from Vancouver Island."

The problem?

The San Juan Islands.

The San Juan Islands form an archipelago, now part of the state of Washington. They sit in the middle of that unnamed "channel" and create three separate "middle" channels. For a dozen years after signing the Oregon Treaty, neither side particularly liked the other's interpretation of which channel was the true divider. The United States preferred the Haro Strait, a channel running west of the archipelago, whereas the UK preferred the Rosario Strait, the channel running to the archipelago's east. This question of ownership caused practical problems. The British Hudson Bay Company set up a sheep ranch on San Juan Island (the largest island in the archipelago of the same name), located between the Haro and Rosario Straits; a few dozen Americans settled there as well.

Lyman Cutlar, an American farmer, was one of those settlers. On June 15, 1859—thirteen years to the day after the two nations signed the Oregon Treaty—Cutlar noticed a pig, owned by Charles Griffin, an employee of the British Hudson Bay Company, eating Cutlar's potato crops. Cutlar considered the pig a trespasser and, angered—this was not the first time this had happened—shot the pig. Cutlar offered Griffin $10 in compensation; Griffin demanded $100. Cutlar withdrew his offer, now believing he was fully within his rights to shoot the (trespassing) pig. Griffin called upon the British authorities to arrest Cutlar. Cutlar and other American settlers, in turn, requested that the American military protect them from the British. Things quickly spiraled out of hand and within two months the forces described above camped on and around San Juan Island, both with strict orders not to fire the first shot. (Opposing troops did, however, toss insults, hoping to coax each other into violating this order.)

Things came to a head when word of the conflict reached Washington, D.C. and London. Both sides wished to keep this conflict bloodless and agreed to jointly occupy San Juan Island peacefully, each with a military base on the island. In 1874, a panel of international arbitrators declared the Haro Strait to be the border and awarded San Juan Island to the United States; the British closed up their base soon thereafter.

BONUS FACT

The military bases from the mid-1800s, now abandoned, have been combined and make up part of San Juan Island National Historic Park. The park is the only U.S. national park that commemorates a British base and the only one where a British flag flies.

BACON OF THE SEA
WHERE PIGS SWIM

The Bahamas is made up of roughly 700 islands scattered southeast of Florida and north of Cuba. One of those islands, Staniel Cay, is a sand-covered reef in the center of the Bahama's Exuma island chain; it is one of the few Exuma islands with a permanent population. Staniel Cay is most notable for two things: Part of the James Bond movie *Thunderball* was filmed there, and it is home to the Staniel Cay Yacht Club, which serves as the nautical center of the immediate vicinity.

That's the only place you'll get to see swimming pigs.

Nearby Staniel Cay is an uninhabited island called Big Majors Spot—uninhabited by people, that is. A bunch of feral cats and a few families of pigs live there. The pigs—being the voracious omnivores pigs are—will eat anything they can find. So when visitors come to the island and toss them apple cores and virtually anything else, the pigs feast.

But these pigs are a bit impatient. Over the years, they and their offspring have learned that the sound of motorboats means that there's food to be had, so the pigs take the initiative—and take to sea. The pigs swim right up to the boats, doggy paddling away, in hopes of obtaining a tasty morsel or two. (You'll find plenty of videos on YouTube if you need to see it to believe it.)

How did pigs get to a small tropical island far from the mainland? We don't know, but there are three possibilities: The pigs ended up there after a shipwreck; farmers came to Big Majors Spot and abandoned their pigs there; or perhaps, residents of Staniel Cay and other inhabited islands put the pigs there as a somewhat underhanded way to fatten them up, on the cheap, before eating them.

In support of that final theory? Attend a celebration at Staniel Cay, and you'll notice pig on the menu.

BONUS FACT

Every so often, pigs make headlines across the United States due to their appearance at McDonald's, in the form of the cult-favorite McRib sandwich. The McRib, a pork patty (from pork shoulder meat, not ribs) slathered in barbecue sauce and covered in onions and pickles, all on a roll, debuted in 1981. It has been a (very successful) promotional item, making limited appearances, since 2006, and whenever news of its arrival leaks, it makes waves on the Internet. But if it weren't for the popularity of Chicken McNuggets, McRib might not have been created. McNuggets, introduced in 1979, were immediately successful, but McDonald's didn't have a large enough supply of chicken to provide them to all franchisees. According to a former McDonald's executive chef in an interview with *MAXIM*, the company created the McRib as an alternative, particularly for Mickey D's in the Midwest.

MCLIBEL
HOW (NOT?) TO SUE MCDONALD'S

Defamation, in the United States, is a difficult legal cause of action in which to prevail, especially if the side making the claim is a public figure or corporation. The First Amendment codifies the right to freedom of speech, which among other things protects Americans' right to engage in debates pertaining to items in the public interest.

But outside the United States there is no First Amendment, and in many cases protections of speech and expressive action are much weaker. In countries such as the United Kingdom a corporation's ability to successfully sue someone for defamation is markedly greater. No one knows this better than Helen Steel and David Morris.

In 1986, a group called "London Greenpeace" (unaffiliated with the well-known group Greenpeace) began distributing a pamphlet in the UK accusing McDonald's of a variety of things, ranging from starving Third World children and poisoning their UK customers to paying low wages and being cruel to chickens and other animals. Over the next few years, McDonald's attempted to infiltrate the group, likely with the intention of finding a way to shut them down.

In 1990, McDonald's identified five of the people spreading the leaflets and brought libel charges against them. Three of the five settled and apologized, rather than incur massive legal fees and put their lives on hold while litigating the question. But Steel and Morris decided that they wanted their day in court. Representing themselves (with some pro bono assistance), the pair spent £30,000 (to McDonald's millions) to defend themselves.

Defending oneself against a UK libel claim is no small task. The burden is on the defendants to prove that each of the claims that they made is, factually, true. Given the number and gravity of Steel and Morris's allegations (assuming they were true in the first place, and who knows?), doing so was virtually impossible. But they tried; they called roughly 180 witnesses during 300 days in court.

And they lost. The court found that although some of their claims were true, such as the accusations of low wages, the pair failed to establish the truth of many other assertions. (The court was unwilling, for example, to grant that McDonald's poisoned its customers.) McDonald's was awarded £60,000, later reduced to £20,000 on appeal—but the victory was a Pyrrhic one. The money was a equivalent to a rounding error, at best, for the multinational restaurant giant. For Steel and Morris, however, it was a ticket to more attention than they'd ever dreamed of receiving. McDonald's became an anathema in many UK communities.

So did the British libel laws. As reported by *The New York Times*, in 2005—nearly two decades after the pamphlets first came out—Steel and Morris sued the British government in the European Court of Human Rights, arguing that the sanctions levied against them violated the European Convention on Human Rights adopted in the 1950s. There, the two prevailed—the Court awarded them £57,000 from the UK government, roughly equal to the amount they owed McDonald's plus their legal costs along the way.

BONUS FACT

In 2003, singer/actress Barbra Streisand sued Kenneth Adelman, a photographer who, in a collection of 12,000 photographs of the California coastline, included an aerial picture of her home in Malibu. She did not simply ask that the photo be removed. According to TechDirt .com, Streisand, citing anti-paparazzi laws, demanded $10 million. The move, however, backfired. Before the lawsuit was filed, the image was downloaded from Adelman's website six times, two of which were from Streisand's lawyers. After news of the filed lawsuit hit? The image was downloaded another 400,000-plus times in that month.

MCHOTDOGS
WHY YOU (PROBABLY) CAN'T GET A HOT DOG AT MCDONALD'S

Fast food has its staples: hamburgers and cheeseburgers, french fries, soda, probably a chicken option such as nuggets or a grilled sandwich. More "exotic" offerings include onion rings, milkshakes, hash browns, and fried fish items. But rarely—Wienerschnitzel franchises excepted—are hot dogs on the menu. For McDonald's, there's a reason. Blame Ray Kroc, the man who bought the tiny company in 1954 and turned it into a multibillion-dollar fast food behemoth.

In 1977, Kroc wrote an autobiography titled *Grinding It Out: The Making Of McDonald's*, documenting his vision for burgers and fries made quickly, cheaply, and on an immense scale. In the book he notes that McDonald's is always experimenting with new potential additions to the menu, going so far as to say that "it's entirely possible that one day we'll have pizza [on the menu]." (Pizza was indeed tested, and made the menu of roughly 500 stores before being withdrawn. According to Wikipedia, though, McPizza was recently available at three McDonald's locations in Spencer, West Virginia, Orlando, Florida, and New Haven, Connecticut.) But Kroc singled out hot dogs as the one food beyond the pale of even experimentation: "On the other hand, there's damned good reason we should never have hot dogs. There's no telling what's inside a hot dog's skin, and our standard of quality just wouldn't permit that kind of item."

Nevertheless, Kroc's edict did not withstand the test of time. McDonald's has tested hot dogs—the McHotDog, naturally—in a number of markets, most notably at the location in Toronto's Sky-Dome (now the Rogers Centre), home of the Toronto Blue Jays. Apparently, in Canada, there's nothing more American than a hot dog at a baseball game.

BONUS FACT

New York City is rife with carts selling hot dogs, pretzels, cold drinks, etc., with the core products running a few bucks, depending on location. Central Park spots can run as high as $175,000 annually, says Yahoo.com, and in 2008, one vendor bid more than $600,000 for the exclusive right to sell wieners outside the Metropolitan Museum of Art.

POTATO PARTIES
WHAT HAPPENS WHEN FRENCH FRIES ARE INCREDIBLY CHEAP

The price of a large order of french fries at a American McDonald's runs about $2.25, give or take a dime or a quarter. The price in Japan is roughly the same—240 yen, or about $2.50. Usually. In the fall of 2012, Japanese Mickey D's ran a promotion advertising large fries for only 150 yen, or about $1.55. The promotion worked better than anyone ever imagined.

Or worse than anyone ever feared—depending on your perspective.

Japanese culture eschews waste, especially when it comes to food. If you put it on your plate, you are expected to finish it, and an order of fries at McDonald's is no exception. At about 500 calories per order, buying two large orders of fries is therefore out of the question, at least if you're eating alone and especially if you have a burger to go with it. But what if you had a group of people? Pooling your money—and your calories—you could probably buy and eat a lot of french fries.

In October of that year, a group of Japanese teens did just that, creating an ad hoc "potato party" by purchasing twenty-three orders of fries and dumping them out across their trays. Normally, this is where the story would end. Even if the store manager made a stink over the gluttony—which would be unlikely to cause a scene, given the Japanese rules of decorum—there is little reason to believe that anyone outside that particular McDonald's would notice. But this was the new normal. The teens did what almost any group of teens in 2012 would do—they took a picture and put it on Twitter. As video game culture blog Kotaku reported, thousands of other East Asian teens noticed and began creating "potato parties" of their own.

These parties were not good for business. Crowds gathered whenever one spontaneously broke out, disrupting the flow of traffic for other customers. Many Japanese saw the behavior as disrespectful, but others fueled the fire as one-upmanship took hold. At the apex, a group of teens ordered sixty portions of large fries. They finished them all and found an audience in the tens of thousands on Twitter in the process.

The potato parties ended in Japan when the 150-yen promotion also came to a halt. Simply put, topping the record of sixty orders of large fries would require well over $150 dollars, a hefty price to pay anywhere. But for some reason, South Koreans had no problem with the price tag. A report on msn.com told the story of teenagers there buying $250 worth of french fries—but without as much success. Many were rebuffed by store managers unwilling to turn their eateries into circuses.

BONUS FACT

In the movie *Pulp Fiction*, Vincent (played by John Travolta) tells Jules (Samuel L. Jackson) that in Paris, the Quarter Pounder with Cheese is called a "Royale with Cheese," because they use the metric system in Europe—it wouldn't make sense to use the term "quarter pound." Vincent was wrong. In France (and, for that matter, in Belgium and Portugal as well), the Quarter Pounder comes with cheese as a standard ingredient, and the whole thing is called a "Royal Cheese." In no country is a Quarter Pounder with Cheese called a "Royale with Cheese."

FIRE HORSE WOMEN
WHY JAPAN'S BIRTH RATE PLUMMETED IN 1966

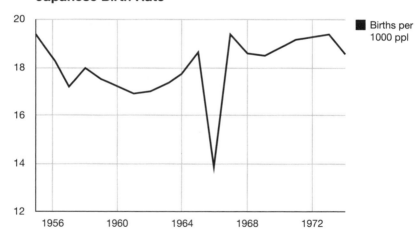

Japanese Birth Rate

■ Births per 1000 ppl

The graph above shows the birth rate in Japan from the twenty-year period beginning in 1955 and ending in 1974. By and large, the curve is relatively stable; give or take, there were between 17 and 19 births per 1,000 people in any given year—except 1966. That year, the birth rate fell to 13.7 births per 1,000 people, easily the lowest during the two-decade period.

What happened? Blame the Fire Horse.

Many Japanese follow the Shengxiao (to Americans, the Chinese zodiac), a series of twelve animals, which rotates annually. Each of the twelve animals has characteristics associated with it—the snake, for example, is said to be intelligent but unscrupulous, whereas the monkey is curious but often headstrong. Every year in late January or early February, as part of the Chinese New Year rituals, the animal of the year changes and people born during the next twelve months or so are thought to have the characteristics of that animal.

Another astrological tradition of the East is the Chinese Wu Xing, or the Five Elements. Each two-year period is associated with one of five things: earth, fire, wood, water, or metal. The Japanese, in particular, use these as modifiers of the Chinese zodiac. A normal "snake" year could become a "water snake" (which was the case in 2013), making the intelligent but unscrupulous person into a less ambitious, somewhat oblivious version of the original. When you multiply the five elements by the dozen zodiac symbols you get sixty combinations, creating, in effect, a sixty-year cycle in both Chinese and Japanese astrology.

Nineteen sixty-six was the year of Hinoe-Uma, or in English, the Fire Horse—a particularly troubling combination for many Japanese would-be parents. (And probably for Chinese would-be parents too, but China doesn't publish demographic data to the extent that Japan does.) People born in the year of the horse, generally, are said to be outgoing and sociable. But the "fire" modifier, legend states, makes them overly ambitious and zealous, willing to sacrifice everything to reach whatever ambition they strive after. In 1966, the culture in Japan made this okay for a boy, but for a girl it was a curse. Fire Horse Women were said to guarantee an early death for both their fathers and husbands, leaving a path of destruction along the way.

One couldn't pick one's child's gender, so the Japanese simply had fewer babies. A report from Yahoo suggested that this wasn't unique to Japan—Korea, Tibet, and China all had fewer births that year as well. There are various reports of increased abstinence, birth control use, and abortions during that year. Further, the graph above demonstrates that this was a multiyear plan for many families, as evidenced by the upticks in the birth rates in the years preceding and following the year of the Fire Horse.

For those East Asian women born in 1966, the Fire Horse brand was for decades an unwelcome one and in many cases, remains so today. Many of those women regularly lie about their birth year, claiming to have been born in 1967. But in recent years, the stigma associated with being a Fire Horse Woman has waned as skepticism over the zodiacal tradition has increased. This is probably a very good thing, as the Year of the Fire Horse comes again in 2026.

BONUS FACT

Over the past few decades, Japan's birth rate has plummeted dramatically but life expectancy has risen. One side effect from the aging population? A change in the diaper business in Japan. According to Bloomberg, Japan's largest diaper maker (a company called Unicharm) sold more adult diapers than baby diapers in 2011—for the first time, ever.

PUMPKIN SAVING TIME
HOW THE CANDY INDUSTRY
CHANGED YOUR CLOCKS

Before 1966, Daylight Saving Time in the United States was set via a patchwork of state and local laws, often causing conflict and confusion. The Uniform Time Act, passed by Congress in 1966, standardized Daylight Saving Time across the nation. As set forth by the act, Daylight Saving Time begins on the last Sunday in April and ends on the last Sunday in October. But the act has been amended twice since. First, in 1986, the beginning of Daylight Saving Time was shifted to the *first* Sunday in April, taking effect the next year. Later, in 2005, both the start and end dates were changed (effective 2007). Daylight Saving Time was to begin a few weeks earlier, at the second Sunday in March, and end a week later than previously, on the first Sunday in November.

Although the second part of the second change seems curious— it pushes Daylight Saving Time's end date back merely a week— one of the forces behind the change is unexpected: candy pumpkins.

The 2005 changes to Daylight Saving Time were purportedly aimed at saving energy (in fact, the amendment is part of a bill called the Energy Policy Act of 2005), but many are skeptical of any such savings. Michael Downing, author of *Spring Forward: The*

Annual Madness of Daylight Saving Time, told NPR that "it turns out every time Congress has studied [Daylight Saving Time], it's been told that we haven't saved anything." Downing continued that any savings from less at-home or at-work energy use is eaten up by additional cars on the road, as people begin to spend their additional natural-daylight leisure time shopping: "The first and most persistent lobby for Daylight Saving in this country was the Chamber of Commerce, because they understood that if their department stores were lit up, people would be tempted by them."

But the Chamber of Commerce was not the only organization lobbying for the extension of Daylight Saving Time. And it was, perhaps, not even the most vocal. That distinction goes to the candy lobby. For them, a one-week move—from the last Sunday in October to the first in November—meant big bucks, as it allowed for an extra hour of trick-or-treating each Halloween.

In 1985, the candy industry made its first attempt to get its desired change enacted with a little bit of bribery—a very little bit. Before the relevant hearing, lobbyists took to the Senate chambers with a bag of candy pumpkins in hand, placing some of the treat on each senator's chair. But Congress returned a trick, keeping the clock rollback date to a time before Halloween. Not until twenty years later, under the 2005 bill, did the candy industry get its desired outcome.

BONUS FACT

Arizona does not follow Daylight Saving Time. However, the Native American Navajo Nation, which sits within Arizona, *does* observe Daylight Saving Time. To make matters more confusing, another Native American tribe, the Hopi Nation, is in an enclave surrounded by the Navajo Nation—and, much like the rest of Arizona, the Hopi Nation *does not* observe Daylight Saving Time.

TRICK OF TREATS
IS HALLOWEEN CANDY REALLY DANGEROUS?

On October 31, 1983, advice columnist Abigail Van Buren—better known as "Dear Abby"—published a Halloween-themed column titled "A Night of Treats, not Tricks." In that column, she wanted to "remind [readers] that," among other things, "[s]omebody's child will become violently ill or die after eating poisoned candy or an apple containing a razor blade." Twelve years later, advice columnist Ann Landers (who, by the way, was Dear Abby's sister) also wrote a Halloween article—"Twisted minds make Halloween a dangerous time"—echoing that concern. "In recent years, there have been reports of people with twisted minds putting razor blades and poison in taffy apples and Halloween candy," Landers wrote. "It is no longer safe to let your child eat treats that come from strangers."

Although there have been reports of razor blades and other foreign objects embedded in Halloween candy (or apples—although anyone giving out an apple on Halloween is already suspect), these dangers are almost always obvious with the most cursory glance. What about poison, which, being invisible and generally hard to detect, is the more nefarious way to taint candy? You have little reason to be concerned there either. Landers stated, "many reports" of such terrible acts have occurred, however, they are almost entirely the stuff of myth.

Almost entirely.

For nearly thirty years, University of Delaware sociologist Joel Best has been investigating allegations of strangers poisoning kids' Halloween candy. As of this writing, he hasn't identified a single confirmed example of a stranger murdering a child in this fashion. He found other examples of people accidentally passing out tainted candy or, in one case, passing out ant poison as a gag gift to teenagers (no one was hurt), but the bogeyman of terrible people making trick-or-treating unsafe is a canard. One example of a person trying, explicitly, to poison children via Halloween candy was confirmed. However, the child who died wasn't a stranger—it was the man's son.

On Halloween, 1974, an eight-year-old boy named Timothy O'Bryan died. His candy had, indeed, been poisoned. A few days prior, his father, Ronald Clark O'Bryan, took out a $40,000 life insurance policy on Timothy and Timothy's sister, Elizabeth (then age five), as an unimaginable way to get out of debt. The only way to collect required that at least one of his children die, so the elder O'Bryan laced some Pixy Stix with cyanide and cajoled his son into eating one before bed.

As murder would negate the insurance policy, the father had to cover his tracks. Already showing a wanton disregard for the lives of others—children, at that—he decided to potentially kill a few. He distributed some of the tainted candy to at least four other children (including his daughter), according to the *Houston Chronicle*, setting up the story that a neighborhood madman or demented factory worker had caused the tragic death of his son. Fortunately, he was unsuccessful. None of the other children ended up eating the poison, in part due to a quick reaction from authorities and in part due to dumb luck—an eleven-year-old tried to eat the sugar in the Pixy Stix he received, but could not undo the staples that O'Bryan had used to reseal the package.

As tragic as this story is, it is the only known example of a person intentionally poisoning Halloween candy and providing it to neighborhood trick-or-treaters. And Ronald Clark O'Bryan won't be poisoning any more candy—the state of Texas executed him in 1984.

BONUS FACT

You probably have some cyanide in your kitchen, and no, it's not in the Pixy Stix or other candy. It's in your fruit bin. The seeds of apples, mangos, and peaches contain trace elements of the poison. (But don't worry—your body can handle small doses of cyanide. You would have to eat a dozen or two apple cores in a single meal in order to feel any meaningful effects.)

ONE-ARMED BANDITS
THE TOWN WHERE ARMS AND LEGS WERE TURNED INTO CASH

According to the FBI, insurance companies collect more than $1 trillion in premiums each year. Also according to the FBI, insurance fraud costs the industry $40 billion annually, causing premiums to increase between $400 and $700 per household. But don't tell that to the people of Vernon, Florida.

Vernon is a small town on Florida's panhandle, not too far from Alabama and Georgia. Its population bounces between 500 and 800, and recently has been rather poor, with one-quarter of the population at or below the poverty line. It's been that way for generations. In the 1950s and 1960s, however, some of the people found a way out of poverty—via a handsome insurance settlement. And it would not cost them an arm and a leg. Just one of the two.

Quite literally, people in Vernon were shooting themselves, blowing off limbs, and collecting on the insurance. How the trend started, no one knows—perhaps it was an accident at a sawmill or with a plow, or perhaps it was a calculated effort to scam an insurance company out of tens of thousands of dollars (or more). Truly, it doesn't matter. For when word got out that so-and-so just received a check for untold riches—and all it cost him was a hand or foot, perhaps even to the elbow or knee—well, the idea spread. By the time the early 1960s rolled around, according to the *Tampa Bay Times*, Vernon, Florida, was responsible for roughly two-thirds of all loss-of-limb-related insurance claims in the United States.

Over the time period in question, a total of fifty people (give or take) lost limbs of some sort, many if not all filing insurance claims thereafter. Although the insurers attempted to bring lawsuit actions against some of these people, not one was convicted of insurance fraud. One alleged transgressor was particularly egregious, but, as the *Times* notes, he avoided conviction and walked away a one-footed millionaire:

> There was another man who took out insurance with 28 or 38 companies," said Murray Armstrong, an insurance official for Liberty National. "He was a farmer and ordinarily drove around the farm in his stick shift pickup. This day—the day of the accident—he drove his wife's automatic transmission car and he lost his left foot. If he'd been driving his pickup, he'd have had to use that foot for the clutch. He also had a tourniquet in his pocket. We asked why he had it and he said, 'Snakes. In case of snake bite.' He'd taken out so much insurance he was paying premiums that cost more than his income. He wasn't poor, either. Middle class. He collected more than $1 million from all the companies. It was hard to make a jury believe a man would shoot off his foot.

A few years later, a filmmaker named Errol Morris came to Vernon, hoping to make a movie (tentatively titled *Nub City*) about the purported scam. But faced with death threats and the like, he instead produced a much less controversial film of the town and named it, cautiously, *Vernon, Florida*. The well-regarded documentary focuses on the town more broadly, bringing to film many eccentricities about the community, but does not focus on the decision of many to dismember themselves.

BONUS FACT

As of 1998, a British insurance company offered policies insuring against alien abduction; $150 would buy you $1.5 million in coverage. The offering company claimed to have sold roughly 20,000 policies.

THE *ZONG*
HISTORY'S WORST INSURANCE FRAUD SCHEME

The *Zong*, a slave ship, set sail from Accra, now the capital of Ghana, on August 18, 1781. It was transporting 442 slaves from Africa to Jamaica, more than it should have been able to carry. The ship made its way across the Atlantic without much incident. When the *Zong* reached the Caribbean island of Tobago, it was in fine enough shape.

Then, everything started to go wrong. The ship failed to dock at Tobago and take on additional supplies. On November 27 or 28, it passed Jamaica, thinking that the island in its sights was Hispanola. The *Zong* sailed farther west into the Caribbean Sea. By the time the crew realized these errors, they simply did not have enough food and water to bring all 442 slaves to Jamaica alive.

So they started to throw them overboard. For the insurance money.

By its very nature, slavery treats people as property. During the slave trade era, insurers sold policies to those involved in the business of shipping people in captivity from Africa to the New World. In the case of the *Zong*, the insurance company would pay the ship's owners £30 for each slave who failed to reach Jamaica in a saleable state. The crew and the ship's human cargo were already suffering from malnutrition, with sixty-two of the 442 slaves already dead. On November 29, just a day or two after overshooting Jamaica, fifty-four African women and children were thrown into the ocean. On December 1, another forty-two slaves—men, this time—met the same fate. This continued over the next few weeks. By the time the *Zong* landed in Jamaica on December 22, only 208 of the slaves—fewer than half—were still on board.

The ship's owners asked their insurer to compensate them for the loss of the 230 or so slaves "lost" at sea, but instead the insurers filed suit. The jury sided with the ship's owners, finding that the slaves were no different than horses and that the ship's captain had the discretion to throw some to their deaths to save the rest.

The insurers appealed. Fortunately, the appellate court found that the captain and crew's mismanagement of the voyage led to the substandard conditions, and further, on December 1, before the forty-two male slaves were thrown overboard, it had rained, which would have alleviated a lot of the water shortages. The appellate court likened the crew's acts to murder (which, to modern ears, this clearly is) and ordered a new trial. There is no evidence that this second trial ever occurred.

The insurer never paid the ship's owners—but that was not the slave merchants' largest loss. The story of the *Zong* massacre would be told repeatedly by abolitionists, as the repugnant acts of the ship's crew and ownership hit a chord with the general public.

BONUS FACT

Hispaniola, the island that the *Zong*'s crew believed Jamaica to be, is now comprised of the countries of Haiti and the Dominican Republic. Haiti is the only modern country that was born from a slave revolt.

THE OVERWATER RAILROAD
THE SLAVE WHO STEAMED TO FREEDOM

One of the more notable strategic decisions of the Civil War was the North's blockade of Confederate ports, cutting the South off from imports, particularly from the Caribbean and Europe. The blockade had mixed success. Smaller, faster ships known as "blockade runners" found it possible to get past the waiting Union navy, with five out of every six ships successfully evading danger. However, the blockade runners were much smaller than the typical cargo ships, and the 500-ship-strong Union blockade managed to destroy 1,500 blockade runners during the course of the war.

The blockade likely also led to the enlistment of African-Americans in the Union army.

On April 12, 1861, the Civil War began as Confederate troops fired on Fort Sumter, a Union stronghold on South Carolina's coastline. Both North and South mobilized their male populations, calling many to arms. But it would not be until January 31, 1863, that the First and Second South Carolina Volunteers, the first African-American battalions, would take to battle for the Union. A mix of bigotry and distrust caused the Northern leadership to delay enlisting African-Americans, and there was the question of whether rank-and-file whites would be willing to fight alongside freedmen or recent slaves.

On the evening of May 12, 1862, the officers of the CSS *Planter*, a Confederate military transport, went ashore for the night. The crew, made up of slaves, was ordered to stay onboard. At 3 A.M. the next morning, led by pilot Robert Smalls, they carried out a daring escape from the South. After commandeering the ship, the crew steamed off to a nearby wharf where their families were hiding, took them aboard, and made their way up the South Carolina coastline. They signaled, as they'd normally do, whenever they passed near a Confederate fort—the forts, therefore, believed their early-morning cruise was nothing out of the ordinary.

After passing Fort Sumter at about 4:30 A.M., Smalls piloted the ship straight toward the Union blockade. The first ship to see the *Planter* was the USS *Onward*, which took aim at the Confederate ship but, seeing the white flag of surrender (a bed sheet) on the mast, boarded it instead. The *Planter* carried four heavy artillery guns, ammunition, and classified documents including a code book and the location of mines within Charleston's harbor. The capture of the *Planter* was a major boon for the Union. Smalls, who would later become a Congressman, quickly became a hero in the North.

Smalls's newfound fame earned him a meeting with Edwin Stanton, the Secretary of War. Smalls used the opportunity to advocate for the enlistment of other African-Americans, seeing service as a way to help bring the former slaves into mainstream society. Smalls was successful. Following the meeting, Stanton issued an order to Smalls, allowing him to enlist up to 5,000 African-Americans in the Union-controlled South Carolina area. Those men became the First and Second South Carolina Volunteers.

BONUS FACT

Officially, the siege of Fort Sumter had a death toll of two men, both Union soldiers. But those deaths weren't at the hands of the Confederacy. Fort Sumter, low on provisions and undermanned, was unable to thwart the Confederate bombardment. Major Robert Anderson, the commander of the fort, agreed to surrender after less than two days of bombardment, under the condition that his men be allowed to give a 100-gun salute when lowering the American flag. During that ceremony, some ammunition went off accidentally, killing privates Edward Galloway and Daniel Hough.

RATS!
HOW VERMIN HELPED BEAT THE NAZIS

As war swept through Europe in the late 1930s and 1940s, it became increasingly clear that the previously genteel methods of killing each other were no longer going to cut it. On June 22, 1940, the British government established a group called the Special Operations Executive (SOE), a secret group of spies charged with finding nontraditional ways to disrupt Nazi plans.

The SOE had roughly 13,000 operatives. Many provided support for other fighters, typically to people fighting in the Resistance; for example, in 1943, four SOE operatives in Greece assisted local freedom fighters in the successful kidnapping of the Nazi governor of Crete. But others were saboteurs—and creative ones at that. Which is why, in 1941, the SEO purchased a hundred or so dead rats, formerly used in medical experiments.

Dead rats generally aren't worth much and, if anything, are a nuisance. (Live rats are probably more so.) This was certainly true for Germans and British alike. Rats had a habit of getting onto trains, and at times, they'd make their way to the boiler room of a steam engine. Firemen, whose job it was to keep tossing coal into the furnace to keep the steam coming, would habitually toss any dead rats into the furnace. So the SOE agents laced these hundred dead rats with a little bit of plastic explosives, enough to sabotage the train and its delivery but not so much as to cause a major disaster (which would cause massive loss of life and prompt an investigation). The rats were then shipped into Germany.

But they were intercepted along the way.

What sounds like a failure, though, turned out to be a success. The Nazis had stopped the first and only shipment of dead rat bombs, but they didn't know that. All dead rats were now suspect, and German firemen had to be on constant lookout for dead rats among the coal heaps.

The SOE concluded that the subsequent drop in efficiency of German trains was a boon, albeit from their perspective, an accidental one. As the *Guardian* would later report, official word from the SOE was that "the trouble caused to [the Nazis] was a much greater success to us than if the rats had actually been used."

BONUS FACT

Hiding explosives in the coal in a train's boiler room isn't new or limited to trains. During the Civil War, the Confederacy developed a device called a "coal torpedo," an explosive-filled iron casting covered in coal. The premise was the same at the rat bombs: The fireman would toss the "torpedo" into the boiler, causing an explosion. The target of the torpedoes were Union steamboats patrolling the south, but we don't know how effective they were—the Confederate powers that be burned most of the official documents of the pseudo-country just before the end of the war.

THE ASSAULT OF AMAGANSETT
WHEN THE NAZIS INVADED AMERICA

With rare exception, American involvement in World War II was focused in Europe and the Pacific. Few acts of war took place on the North American continent, a function primarily of the United States's geographic isolation. But this did not keep the Germans from attempting to bring the war Stateside. In fact, on June 13, 1942, four German operatives landed at Amagansett, New York, near the eastern tip of Long Island. Three days later, another four Nazis came ashore at Ponte Vedra Beach, Florida, just south of Jacksonville.

Their orders? To wreak havoc on America's infrastructure.

The eight were trained as saboteurs and given targets: hydro-electric plants, a chemical plant, shipping locks in the Ohio River, and, of particular note, the railway industry. Hell Gate Bridge in New York, a four-track bridge that allowed for the transport of both passengers and freight across the East River bordering Manhattan, was specifically targeted, as was Newark, New Jersey's main train station. Horseshoe Curve, a railroad pass in central Pennsylvania that connected the Pittsburgh steel industry to the industrialized population east, was also on the list of places to be sabotaged, as were the Pennsylvania Railroad's nearby repair yards. Had the plan succeeded, America's industrial complex would have stalled.

The plot failed when two of the conspirators instead attempted to defect. George Dasch, who headed up the team, went to the FBI in Washington, D.C., instead of to his German-assigned target. He attempted to turn himself in and, with co-conspirator Ernst Burger (an American citizen), told the FBI about the plot. However, the two were written off as mere nutcases. Dasch was not to be ignored, however. He returned to the FBI, dropped over $80,000 on the desk—money he received to execute the planned sabotage—and was taken seriously. After hours of interrogation, Burger and the other six Nazis were arrested.

Justice was swift. In July, all eight would-be saboteurs—including Dasch—were convicted of various war crimes and sentenced to death by electrocution. On August 8, 1942, six of the eight were indeed executed, but Burger and Dasch were spared. President Roosevelt commuted Burger's sentence to life in prison and Dasch's to thirty years. Six years later (after the war), President Truman granted clemency to both so long as they accepted deportation to American-occupied Germany.

The two lived out their remaining days—Burger lived to be sixty-nine years old, Dasch died at age eighty-nine—as men without a country. The United States viewed them as enemy combatants, never issuing them a pardon, whereas the pair's German compatriots viewed them as traitors who turned on their fellow soldiers.

BONUS FACT

The men above weren't the only German spies to invade the United States—nor were they the only ones foiled when a compatriot turned himself in. On November 29, 1944, Erich Gimpel (a German) and

William Colepaugh (an American who had defected to Nazi Germany earlier that year) were brought to Maine via U-boat. Their orders were to gather intelligence (perhaps to investigate American work on atomic weapons), not to blow anything up. But the plan failed. Colepaugh abandoned the mission, met up with friends in the States, and ultimately turned himself into the FBI. Both he and Gimpel were sentenced to death. Their sentences were commuted to life in prison and they were released on parole by 1960.

WAR GAMES
HOW MONOPOLY AND PLAYING CARDS FREED POWS

During World War II, Nazi Germany took many prisoners of war (POWs), as is common in warfare. Nazi concentration camps were the scenes of endless horrors, but POW camps were relatively humane (again, relatively). The Nazis even allowed the home nations of the POWs to send them mail. Specifically, the Nazis allowed the Allies to send care packages to those imprisoned, which included items such as playing cards and board games.

The Allies used this minor bit of hospitality to their strategic advantage.

The United States worked with the United States Playing Card Company to come up with a special type of Bicycle-brand playing cards. Those cards held escape maps within them, printed directly on the cards. As recounted by the company's official website, when moistened, the cards' glue—a special type of glue used for this purpose—would weaken. The cards' faces would peel away, revealing detailed escape plans.

The United Kingdom pulled off a similar trick. In 1941, British intelligence worked with John Waddington Ltd., the UK company licensed to make Monopoly games, to produce a special version of the classic board game. According to *Mental Floss* magazine, these sets came with a cornucopia of clandestine goodies. Maps, printed on silk to avoid destruction by weather, were hidden within the box. The games also included metal files and magnetic compasses to facilitate an escape. And included beneath the Monopoly money was real money—French, German, and Italian notes were among the fake bills.

These board games would be collectors' items today, but unfortunately finding one would be a trick all to itself. All the spy-enhanced Monopoly sets were destroyed after the war, according to *ABC News*.

BONUS FACT

Playing cards had a role in the Vietnam War as well. The Viet Cong were apparently superstitious and fearful of the Ace of Spades, which was previously used by French fortune-tellers in the area to signify death. American commanders requested decks full of only the Ace of Spades, and Bicycle, of course, provided them (for free). American troops left the cards in strategic places, and some Viet Cong would flee upon seeing what they believed was a bad omen.

MISSILE MAIL
A REALLY QUICK WAY TO DELIVER THE MAIL

Norfolk, Virginia is about 600 or so miles from Jacksonville, Florida. Depending on what route you take and how fast you drive, it would take you about nine or ten hours to deliver a piece of mail—say, a postcard—from one city to the other. If you took a plane, assuming you weren't held up in security or delayed on the tarmac, it would take just over an hour and a half. That's pretty good, but for decades, postal authorities aspired to deliver the mail faster. Much faster.

And in 1959, the U.S. Postal Service managed to deliver 3,000 pieces of mail from the Norfolk area to Jacksonville in twenty-two minutes. How?

It put them on a nuclear missile.

In the early 1930s and into the 1940s, many postal services were experimenting with the idea of using rocketry as a way to expedite mail delivery. The first known attempts were in Austria in 1931, but the experiments failed to yield long-term use. Around the same time, a German businessman and rocket scientist named Gerhard Zucker became an evangelist for the idea, traveling around both Germany and the United Kingdom to find an audience for his ideas. He ran some test flights in the south of England with mixed results; some of the envelopes exploded along with one of the rockets, but another flight successfully delivered the test mail. No one bought Zuckers's service, but others tried to recreate it themselves.

The United States made its first attempt at what would later be termed "rocket mail" in 1936, firing a pair of rockets across a lake on the border of New York and New Jersey. But the distance— only about 1,000 feet—wasn't very impressive. A couple decades later, the Post Office Department (now the U.S. Postal Service) decided to try and make it work, for real. On June 8, 1959, working with the U.S. Navy, they fired a nuclear missile from the USS *Barbero*, a submarine then stationed a few miles off the coast of Norfolk. The nuclear warhead had been replaced with 3,000 postal covers—basically, commemorative envelopes with precancelled stamps—containing letters from Postmaster General Arthur Summerfield. The letters were addressed to President Eisenhower and a series of governmental and postal officials throughout the United States, and all had the same return address: "The Postmaster General, Washington."

The missile took flight at 9:30 A.M. Its guidance system was programmed to land at Naval Station Mayport, a military airport a few miles east of Jacksonville, situated on a harbor in Florida. At approximately 9:52, it successfully landed at Mayport. The mission was a success. Postmaster General Summerfield proclaimed that "before man reaches the moon, mail will be delivered within hours from New York to California, to Britain, to India or Australia by guided missiles. We stand on the threshold of rocket mail."

He was obviously wrong. Most experts believe that "rocket mail" is too expensive to justify the otherwise very cool idea.

BONUS FACT

The Postmaster General isn't a general. Neither are the Surgeon General or any of the Attorneys General, for that matter. "General," in these contexts, is not a noun but an adjective, showing the expansiveness of the postmaster's (or surgeon's or attorney's) expertise. According to Michael Herz, a professor of law at the Benjamin N. Cardozo School of Law in New York, who investigated the question insofar as "attorney general" is concerned, there's no basis for calling these governmental leaders "generals." Says Herz, doing so is "flatly incorrect by the standards of history, grammar, lexicology and protocol."

SPACE MAIL
HOW SOME APOLLO *ASTRONAUTS MADE MONEY ON THE SIDE*

An old postage stamp cover might not strike you as very exciting. But in at least several cases, those covers have been somewhere you'll probably never go: the moon. And there's a very good chance that many of these special envelopes shouldn't have gone to the moon in the first place. The fact that some of them did may have cost a couple astronauts their jobs.

Apollo 15 launched from Kennedy Space Center in Florida on July 26, 1971. Its lunar module landed on the moon's surface four days later. The spacecraft carried three astronauts—Commander David Scott, Lunar Module Pilot James Irwin, and Command Module Pilot Alfred Worden—and 641 postage stamp covers. Of those 641, 243 were authorized by NASA, a common way for space missions at the time to create collectables marking the historic occasions. (Most likely, 250 were authorized, but miscounting or damage to some covers reduced the number actually brought into space to 243.) The other 398—400, minus two that were damaged and therefore discarded—were smuggled aboard.

Before the *Apollo 15* mission launch, a German stamp collector named Herman Sieger found out about the 243

NASA-authorized stamp covers and saw an opportunity. He connected with a German man (and naturalized American citizen) named Walter Eiermann, who was well known in the area around Kennedy Space Center and had many contacts within NASA. He convinced the three astronauts to bring the extra 398 stamp covers aboard the flight with them, offering them $7,000 for their troubles, and giving them an extra 100 covers for their own purposes. Scott, who was traveling with an authorized cancellation stamp (for the 243 preapproved covers), was to cancel the 398 contraband covers upon the mission's return to Earth.

That part of the plan went without a hitch. The stamp covers made the trip and were returned to Sieger, who had originally agreed to not sell any of the stamp covers until after the final Apollo mission came to a close (which, as it turns out, would be another year and a half or so). But Sieger failed to keep that part of the bargain. As reported by the *Spokesman-Review*, he started to sell them almost immediately after, receiving $1,500 for each. In total, he earned roughly $300,000 (about $1.6 million in today's dollars, accounting for inflation)—which, of course, caught the eye of critics far and wide.

Even though what the astronauts did was not illegal, many objected, seeing the noble heroes become nothing more than profiteering opportunists. (Irwin, by some reports, would later say that he was simply trying to earn enough money to pay for his children's college educations.) Congress ordered NASA to take action. NASA reassigned the astronauts to nonflight roles and confiscated their 100 remaining covers, prompting their resignations.

A few years later, in 1983, NASA and the U.S. Postal Service partnered to put 260,000 commemorative stamp covers on the STS-8 *Challenger* shuttle mission. Noting that what they did was not very different, the *Apollo 15* crew took legal action to regain their own stamp covers. According to Worden's autobiography, they settled with NASA and the covers were returned. As recently as 2011, one of the covers sold at auction for $15,000.

BONUS FACT

Worden has two claims to fame due to the *Apollo 15* mission. On August 5, 1971, he made the first walk in deep space, 196,000 miles from Earth; from that vantage point, he was able to see both the moon and Earth, as he told CNN. Second, Worden holds the record for the most isolated known person in human history. While Scott and Irwin were on the moon's surface, Worden was in orbit above the moon, alone, and at one point was 2,235 miles away from the two men on the surface below. (That's roughly the distance from Barcelona to Moscow.)

STAR-SPANGLED
MOON BANNERS
WHAT HAPPENED TO THE FLAGS ON THE MOON?

On July 20, 1969, Neil Armstrong and Buzz Aldrin became the first people to set foot on the moon. As part of the *Apollo 11* mission, they famously took a flag pole mounted with an American flag and placed it on the moon's surface next to a plaque that read "Here men from the planet Earth first set foot upon the moon, July 1969 A.D. We came in peace for all mankind." The flag's placement was broadcast back to the rest of us on Earth. More than a half-century later—and no human has returned to the massive rock orbiting our planet in more than forty years—that remains one of the most iconic images of the twentieth century.

The flag? It's almost certainly not there anymore. (And no, aliens did not take it.)

Each of the Apollo missions left an American flag on the moon. When the *Apollo 11* crew planted theirs, though, they made one of the few notable (but arguably insignificant) errors of the mission—they placed it too close to the lunar lander. When Armstrong and Aldrin took off from the moon to rejoin Michael Collins in the command module in the lunar orbiter, Aldrin realized the error. As he'd later recount, he saw the flag fall over as the lander's rockets fired, and assumed that the nylon flag was vaporized in the process. We can't be sure, but that's the most likely scenario.

For decades, NASA experts and other researchers believed that, if anything, this minor faux pas had little to no effect on anything, because they generally believed that the flags left behind would have crumbled into space dust (or whatever space items turn into over time) within a few years of their placement. But that turns out to be wrong. The flags—except for *Apollo 11*'s—are still there.

In 2009, NASA launched the Lunar Reconnaissance Orbiter (LRO), an unmanned spacecraft that still orbits the moon, taking pictures of its surface along the way. The LRO is programmed to take pictures of each of the Apollo landing sites and, in 2012, picked up shadows near each site. The flags, NASA concluded, are causing those shadows.

So they are almost certainly still there. But they aren't very American anymore.

The colors on nylon fade over time, and a nylon American flag on Earth, set outside somewhere for forty or fifty years, would be washed out—closer to pink, white, and azure than red, white, and blue. The same item on the moon, though, would fade much more quickly, because the moon doesn't have an atmosphere, and therefore, the sun's UV rays hit the surface uninhibited.

It is widely agreed that the flags on the moon are, therefore, blanched white—except for *Apollo 11*'s, which was probably vaporized.

BONUS FACT

The *Apollo 11* flag appeared to be waving in the wind, which is impossible, because there is no wind on the moon. What happened? Another error (with a neat result) caused the illusion. To get the flag to the moon, NASA furled it up in a heat-resistant tube. NASA outfitted the top and the bottom of the flag with telescoping arms that, when Armstrong unfurled the flag, were supposed to extend. But the bottom one didn't fully do so, creating a permanent ripple in the flag (until it was likely vaporized when Armstrong and Aldrin departed, of course).

MAROONED ON THE MOON
WHAT WOULD HAVE HAPPENED IF NEIL ARMSTRONG AND BUZZ ALDRIN WERE STRANDED ON THE MOON?

Sometimes, the grandest plans go awry. And because of that, we often plan for the worst-case scenario.

When Neil Armstrong and Buzz Aldrin disembarked from the lunar lander in the summer of 1969, they became the first people ever to walk on the moon. The landing, according to NASA, was not the troubling part. Rather, NASA's biggest concern was whether the lunar lander would be able to leave the moon's surface and return to the lunar orbiter, piloted and manned by Michael Collins, awaiting them for the return to Earth. If the lunar lander's liftoff failed, both Armstrong and Aldrin would be marooned on the moon, with the world watching on television.

Then-President Richard M. Nixon's speechwriter, William Safire (who would later become a *New York Times* columnist), took it upon himself to draft a plan and a message from Nixon in case of this disaster. That message outlined the plan. First, Nixon would call (in Safire's words) the "widows-to-be," offering the nation's condolences. Then, communications with the moon would be cut, and a member of the clergy would offer a prayer similar to one used for a burial at sea, and close with the Lord's

Prayer. Finally, Nixon would read the following statement to those watching on television:

Fate has ordained that the men who went to the moon to explore in peace will stay on the moon to rest in peace.

These brave men, Neil Armstrong and Edwin Aldrin, know that there is no hope for their recovery. But they also know that there is hope for mankind in their sacrifice.

These two men are laying down their lives in mankind's most noble goal: the search for truth and understanding. They will be mourned by their families and friends; they will be mourned by their nation; they will be mourned by the people of the world; they will be mourned by a Mother Earth that dared send two of her sons into the unknown.

In their exploration, they stirred the people of the world to feel as one; in their sacrifice, they bind more tightly the brotherhood of man.

In ancient days, men looked at stars and saw their heroes in the constellations. In modern times, we do much the same, but our heroes are epic men of flesh and blood.

Others will follow, and surely find their way home. Man's search will not be denied. But these men were the first, and they will remain the foremost in our hearts.

For every human being who looks up at the moon in the nights to come will know that there is some corner of another world that is forever mankind.

The address was never used, and it's unclear if Nixon himself ever knew of its existence until well afterward. The astronauts, however, did learn of it. In 1999, in celebration of the thirtieth anniversary of the successful moon landing, the late Tim Russert had Aldrin, Armstrong, and Collins on *Meet the Press* and read the statement to them.

BONUS FACT

On June 6, 1944, Allied forces successfully pulled off the now-famous D-Day landing on Normandy Beach, France, a tide-turning victory in World War II. Had it failed, then-General Dwight D. Eisenhower was prepared to issue a statement:

Our landings in the Cherbourg-Havre area have failed to gain a satisfactory foothold and I have withdrawn the troops. My decision to attack at this time and place was based on the best information available. The troops, the air, and the Navy did all that bravery and devotion to duty could do. If any blame or fault attaches to the attempt it is mine alone.

Having a lot on his mind, he dated the draft incorrectly—it reads "July 5." He threw the paper aside when it became clear that the invasion was a success, but a historically aware assistant realized the value of the document and retained it. And it would come up again two decades later: Safire cited Eisenhower's decision to draft a worst-case-scenario statement as his reason to do the same for the moon landing.

D-DAY'S DOOMED DRY RUN
THE PRACTICE D-DAY INVASION THAT WENT TERRIBLY WRONG

On June 6, 1944—D-Day—the fate of World War II hung in the balance as Allied forces attempted to liberate Nazi-occupied France. More than 150,000 troops crossed the English Channel that day aboard nearly 7,000 ships supported by 12,000 planes, landing on a series of beaches in Normandy, France. By the end of August, more than 3 million Allied troops were in France. D-Day and the larger Battle of Normandy were decisive victories for the Allies and on August 25, 1944, the Germans surrendered control of Paris back to the French.

But D-Day almost never happened.

American General Dwight D. Eisenhower, the commander of the Supreme Headquarters Allied Expeditionary Force, led the U.S. and UK troops in northwest Europe. In this role, he assumed command of the planned D-Day invasion. He wanted to do everything possible to make sure it would work, so he ordered a practice called Exercise Tiger. A beach called Slapton in the south of Great Britain was to be the staging ground for a faux invasion, with the assault coming from across Lyme Bay directly to Slapton's east. The roughly 3,000 people living in the area were evacuated and on the evening of April 26, 1944, Allied troops began their "assault" on the beach. It did not go so well.

The plan was to make the dry run "invasion" as realistic as possible, so gunships were to shell the test beach starting at 6:30 A.M. on April 27 for thirty minutes. At 7:30 A.M., landing ships would drop off the soldiers and tanks. At that point, the artillery would fire live ammunition well over the heads of the troops landing, much as they would be doing during an actual invasion. However, some of the landing ships were delayed, which in turn delayed the artillery fire. The battle cruiser received the orders to wait until 7:30, but some of the landing parties were not similarly instructed to wait until 8:30 to disembark. Some Marines lost their lives as they raided the beach at 7:30, just as the cruiser opened fire.

Then it got worse. The next day, nine German E-boats happened upon Lyme Bay. British sentries detected these enemy fast-assault ships but opted to let them through rather than give away the location and size of Allied fortifications in the area. Instead, the British commanders radioed ahead to the HMS *Azalea*, a warship escorting a convoy of nine American LSTs (landing ships carrying tanks) through the bay. The American and British forces, however, were using different radio frequencies. The HMS *Azalea* believed that the LSTs knew about the E-boats, but they didn't. The LSTs' lone escort was insufficient to repel the attack and the LSTs were, colloquially, sitting ducks. Two of the nine LSTs were sunk and another two were damaged before the other LSTs could effectively return fire and force the E-boats to retreat. Many soldiers jumped into the water but put on their life jackets incorrectly; as a result the jackets worked more like anchors than floatation devices. All told, nearly 1,000 men died. Decades later, Steve Sadlon, a radio operator from the first LST attacked, described the carnage to MSNBC. He jumped off his ship, aflame, into the English Channel. He spent four hours in the cold water until he was rescued, unconscious from hypothermia. His memories of the day are harrowing:

It was an inferno . . . The fire was circling the ship. It was terrible. Guys were burning to death and screaming. Even to this day I remember it. Every time I go to bed, it pops into my head. I can't forget it . . . Guys were grabbing hold of us and we had to fight them off. Guys were screaming, 'Help, help, help' and then you wouldn't hear their voices anymore.

From a macro perspective, the E-boat attack caused a massive strategic problem. The actual D-Day invasion was supposed to be a surprise. Now the military had to figure out how to keep the deaths of nearly 1,000 soldiers under wraps. This was done via threat of court martial. Subordinate soldiers were informed that families were being told that the dead were simply missing in action, and any discussion of the tragic two days was patently disallowed.

But even this was not enough. Ten of the men who went missing due to the E-boat attacks knew details of the D-Day invasion plans. Initially, Eisenhower and the rest of Allied leadership decided to delay the actual invasion, fearing that if any of those ten men were captured by the Germans, the enemy could obtain intel about the otherwise secret plan. Not until their bodies were discovered did the D-Day plan go back into action—with improved life jacket training and a single radio frequency for both American and British forces.

For decades after Exercise Tiger, the story went mostly untold. Before D-Day it was a secret; after D-Day it was old news. But in 1984, a resident of the Slapton Beach area managed to raise a sunken tank from Lyme Bay and turn it into a war memorial, with a plaque describing the tragedy.

BONUS FACT

The only general to land at Normandy by sea with the first wave of troops was Theodore Roosevelt Jr., the son of former president Teddy

Roosevelt. He was also the only American to fight at Normandy along-side his son—Theodore Jr. was fifty-six, and his fourth child, Quentin Roosevelt II (named after his late uncle), was a twenty-four-year-old captain at the time of the invasion.

IF DAY
THE NAZIS'S ONE-DAY INVASION OF CANADA

On February 19, 1942, the Nazis invaded Winnipeg, the capital and largest city of the Canadian province of Manitoba. Thirty-five hundred troops entered the city starting at 5:30 A.M., just hours after a one-hour blackout as fighter planes flew over the city in an apparent bombing run. More bombers followed at around 7 A.M., and by 9:30 that morning the few Canadian troops in the area surrendered. The province's premier, the mayor of Winnipeg, and other officials were sent to an internment camp about seventeen miles north-northeast of the city. The leader of the invaders, a man named Erich von Neurenberg, took control of the province. He issued a decree turning Manitoba into a *de facto* police state.

According to von Neurenberg's decree, Manitoba was now part of Nazi Germany—the "Greater Reich," as the document stated—and everyone was subject to the whims of the Germans. A strict curfew was established; Manitobans were not allowed out from 9:30 P.M. until daybreak the next day, and public places were shuttered to citizens altogether. Gatherings of more than eight people were barred, even in private; households were required to provide lodging for up to five German soldiers. Many private organizations were disbanded and the Boy Scouts were made a sub-organization of the Nazis. Farmers were required to sell everything—even things they'd consume themselves—through a central authority. All cars, trucks, and buses were to be forfeited to the "Army of the Occupation." Any attempts to leave or enter Manitoba, organize resistance to the occupiers, or hide any goods from the Nazis (or possess a weapon, hidden or otherwise) was punishable by death, without trial.

And then, at 5:30 P.M. that same day, the occupation ended. It was fake.

In order to fund Canada's part of the war, the country did what many nations opted to do and issued war bonds. The war bonds were, effectively, loans to the government that would allow for additional spending in the war effort. Manitoba was expected to raise $45 million (Canadian) in the effort; Winnipeg itself was responsible for more than half of that. To encourage the purchase of "Victory Bonds," as they were called, a group called the Greater Winnipeg Victory Loan Organization devised a plan. They broke the city up into forty-five districts and initiated the fake invasion. Citizens of Winnipeg and those of neighboring towns were alerted to the ruse a few days beforehand—scaring people to death was not the goal here—and how to escape the rule of the faux Nazis. When your district raised a preset target amount for the Victory Bonds effort, you and your neighbors went free.

Although the "occupation" was only going to last a day, the Victory Loan Organization pulled few punches. Churches were barred from holding services. Armed soldiers searched buses. One of the principals of a local elementary was "arrested" and replaced by a Nazi propagandist. There was even a book burning in front of the city library. (The books used were scheduled to be destroyed anyway; they had fallen into disrepair.)

The event, called "If Day" in the press, was a fundraising success. The Victory Bonds effort raised C$3.2 million from Winnipeg that day alone—in today's dollars, that's about $40 million (U.S. dollars) from a city of about 250,000 at the time. Manitoba as a whole raised C$60 million—33 percent more than its target amount—during the fundraising month. However, If Day failed in another capacity: recruitment. Roughly three dozen men signed up daily to join the war effort during the weeks before If Day, but only about twenty to twenty-five signed up on If Day itself.

BONUS FACT

Winnie the Pooh is, indirectly, named after the city of Winnipeg. Christopher Robin Milne, the son of author A. A. Milne, had a stuffed teddy bear that he named Winnie, upon which the character is based. But Winnie (the teddy bear) was originally named Edward. During the First World War, a British cavalry regiment smuggled a Canadian brown bear into London, donating it to the London Zoo. The cavalry's veterinarian was from Manitoba and named the bear Winnipeg after his hometown. Over time, "Winnipeg" became "Winnie." Christopher Milne became fond of the zoo's new attraction and renamed his teddy bear after it. (The "Pooh" part? Pooh was a swan.)

UNHIP TO BE SQUARE
THE BEST MARKETING SCHEME
YOU'VE NEVER HEARD OF

Shreddies is a brand of breakfast cereal common in the UK and Canada. The cereal is comprised of squares, similar in size and design to Chex in America, and is made from whole wheat. Shreddies come in a variety of flavors, but nothing terribly out of the ordinary as far as cereal is concerned. It is a reliable yet milquetoast breakfast option and has been since 1939.

Which creates a problem for those who are charged with growing sales for the product. How do you make a half-century-old, tried-and-true product seem new or different?

For years, Shreddies' ad men had achieved limited success advertising a bland product. For years, they successfully positioned the brand using the tagline "Keeps Hunger Locked Up Until Lunch," a straightforward appeal to everyday hunger. In 2007, they launched a TV ad campaign featuring a factory of grandmothers—who better to show the wholesome goodness promised by a generations-old product?—knitting lattices of whole wheat together. Like many other cereals, at times, the boxes had toys inside (often *Tom and Jerry* stickers). Through these the manufacturers hoped to give parents an added reason for purchasing the cereal (or, for the cynics, reasons for the children to ask for it).

All fine, but nothing really interesting. Until 2009, when an intern at Post Foods Canada suggested that the brand shake things up. Or, more accurately, spin things a bit. The marketing campaign? A whole new product—Diamond Shreddies—created by an accident at their factories.

The product, of course, was exactly the same—a diamond is just a square, rotated bit. But the public wasn't sure. Post approached the product launch the way one would expect a launch for a "new and improved" product: with a multimedia ad campaign trumpeting the difference. Square Shreddies were "Old (Boring)" whereas the Diamond ones were "New (Exciting!)." TV commercials showed prank market research panels, with members trumpeting the much more tasty diamond ones. Regular square Shreddies were pulled from the shelves in favor of new boxes of Diamond Shreddies; "researchers" asked purchasers to vote for their preferred shape-slash-product at a now-defunct website DiamondOrSquare.com. Some people, playing along, preferred the old square product. So as a final coup de grace, Post responded to the traditionalists in the crowd and released a Diamond Shreddies "Combo Pack"—both square and Diamond Shreddies combined (mixed?) in the same box.

The tongue-in-cheek ad campaign worked. As *MacLeans* reported, the promotion resulted in a measurable and significant increase in sales.

BONUS FACT

If there's one breakfast staple more common than cereal, coffee probably deserves the honor. But coffee hasn't always played that role, at least not in Europe. According to a report by *National Geographic*, the use of coffee (and tea) in the West only began around the time of the Industrial Revolution. Before then, the breakfast drink of choice, per *Nat Geo*, was beer.

LIMONANA
WHEN LIFE GIVES YOU ADVERTISING SPACE, MAKE LEMONADE

Lemonade is a summer staple in the United States and elsewhere, and few would object to calling it the unofficial drink of the season. It comes in many varieties and combinations and for many schoolchildren, provides temporary summer employment. The nickel or quarter a glass lemonade stand, one could fairly assert, is the first business experience of generations of marketing and advertising professionals.

But in one case, the professionals came before the lemonade.

Limonana is a type of lemonade common in the Middle East. It's made of lemon juice mixed with ground mint leaves and sweeteners added to taste. The combination, which is typically made fresh, made its way into the public eye in the 1990s, when an advertising agency in Israel crafted a campaign depicting local celebrities drinking the green lemonade. The ads, which were displayed exclusively on public buses, worked. Thirsty Israelis went to their vendors of choice, asking for their first taste of limonana.

For the storekeepers, this request proved difficult. Limonana, it turned out, didn't exist. The ad agency had made it up.

Public buses have been a staple method of transportation in Israel for most of its history, but skepticism about using them to advertise products was very high. Unconvinced advertisers were, understandably, slow to pony up their money for the ad space, likely frustrating the agencies that believed in the value on the outside of, and inside of, buses. One agency, named Fogel Levin, took matters into its own hands, buying ad space in the hope of proving that it had value.

Then, the agency invented the product. It concocted the fake limonana product (or, at least, gave it a name; the mixture probably was a folk recipe) and promoted it, inking an endorsement with a soccer player named Eli Ohana ("Ohana drinks Limonana"), a man widely regarded to be one of the best Israelis in the game. Other endorsements for the fictional product followed, and in two weeks' time, Israelis were hooked, insisting that they be allowed to drink it, too.

Vendors agreed. The name "limonana" is descriptive—"limon" is the Hebrew and Arabic word for "lemon," and "nana" is the word for "mint" in both languages. The most common recipe is exactly what one would expect given the lack of instruction: a straightforward mint-flavored lemonade. (Why would-be purchasers did not simply make the stuff at home is anyone's guess.) And with that, a product was born.

Limonana is now found throughout Israel and its neighboring countries—and, in a few cafes in the United States and Canada as well. And bus advertising in Israel has become commonplace.

BONUS FACT

Lemonade may help stave off kidney stones, according to the University of California San Diego's Kidney Stone Center. Although all citrus fruits contain a citric acid derivative called citrate, lemons have the highest concentration of it, and citrate slows the creation of kidney stones. A UCSD study showed that drinking four ounces of lemon juice (diluted in two liters of water) each day reduced kidney stone formation by more than 80 percent.

A DATE WITH DESTINY
THE EXTINCT TREE THAT CAME BACK TO LIFE

The last sighting of a dodo bird was in 1662. It is probably the quintessential example of an extinct species. The dodo is long gone, dead—never to return. And in general, that is what "extinct" means.

But sometimes, an exception occurs—such is the case of the Judean date palm.

The Judean Desert extends, roughly, from Jerusalem to the Dead Sea. As the name implies, not a lot of flora grow in the area. But up until about 1,500 to 2,000 years ago, a tree called the Judean date palm was generally plentiful in the area. The tree, which became the symbol of the region roughly 2,500 to 3,000 years ago, provided fruit (dates) to the people in the area as well as shade and shelter. When the Romans captured the region and destroyed the second Jewish Temple in the year 70, the Roman emperor Vespasian minted a coin called the "Judaea Capta." The back of the Capta depicts a Judean date palm, demonstrating how prevalent the tree was in the area.

Yet soon after it vanished. Exports of the dates ended under Roman rule, and sometime before the year 500 the Judean date palm disappeared from the area—and, therefore, the world.

The tree would have been lost forever but for one thing. An early Roman ruler of the area, Herod the Great, built a fortress on top of a mesa called Masada about a century before the destruction of the Second Temple. Masada still exists today (and, in fact, is one of Israel's top tourists attractions). In the mid-1960s, excavators working on the site found some seeds well preserved in ancient pottery. Using carbon-dating techniques, researchers determined that the seeds were 1,900 to 2,000 years old. They kept the seeds in storage for forty years until they could plant them with reasonable success of germination, and in 2005, did exactly that. The seeds were placed in a special, hormone-infused soil.

Eight weeks later, one of the seeds sprouted. By 2010, the young tree had reached a height of two meters tall, and the Judean date palm returned from the land of the dodo. Today, the tree—male—lives on a kibbutz in southern Israel. Plans are being made to mate it with a female tree of another species, in hopes of developing fruit by the mid-2020s.

BONUS FACT

Over the past few decades, China has taken many steps to protect existing forests while encouraging the planting of new trees. In 1999, for example, the government banned the cutting down of trees in natural forests, and, as recently as 2010, China has invested more than $8 billion annually in planting new trees. It is one of two nations that have had a net gain in the number of trees thus far in the (admittedly young) twenty-first century. The other? Israel. The mostly desert landscape now has 240 million trees, according to the Jewish National Fund, which coordinates tree planting throughout the country, allowing anyone (even people outside of Israel) to fund the planting of a tree—one for $18 or three for $36.

SUPER SEED BANK
HOW WE PREVENT THE ERADICATION OF PLANT SPECIES

Imagine a monstrous building embedded in the ice and snow of a Norwegian island in the Arctic Circle. The building resembles something out of *The Empire Strikes Back*—perhaps an entrance to the secret Rebel base on the ice planet of Hoth. Like the Hoth base, the structure is designed to hide important things from danger. But unlike the *Empire* storyline, the things being protected are not people.

They're seeds.

The building? It is the Svalbard Global Seed Vault, the world's largest repository of these potential plants.

There are about 1,400 seed banks throughout the world, each keeping a set of seeds of flora of their regions. The goal of these seed banks is to make sure that we can replant virtually anything that would otherwise be lost to antiquity, be it due to disuse, natural disaster, war, etc. So long as there are seeds in the seed bank, there is always a chance for renewal.

But although a lot of seed banks exist, not a lot of duplication was considered when assembling them. Plants indigenous to only one region may have had their seeds "backed up" only in that area's seed bank—if anything were to happen to the region, the seed bank could be destroyed. Though uncommon, this is not unheard of; as the *Associated Press* noted, seed banks in both Iraq and Afghanistan were casualties of war, whereas one in the Philippines was destroyed during the 2006 typhoon there. Recognizing that localized seed banks were inadequate, a number of NGOs worked with the government of Norway to create the Svalbard Global Seed Vault.

The vault, costing a total of $9 million, is less than 1,000 miles from the North Pole. Built into a sandstone mountain, its entrance leads down a nearly 400-foot corridor into where the vaults themselves are situated. The location was chosen because it provides an unusual combination of environmental factors. First, there is little to no tectonic activity in the area, making an earthquake extremely unlikely. Second, the vault is situated so far above sea level (more than 400 feet) that even the melting of the ice caps would keep it out of reach of floods. Finally, the permafrost in the area helps keep the vault cool, allowing the seeds to stay preserved for an extended time even if the vault loses power. It's called, colloquially, the doomsday vault—and for very good reason. If everything were to go wrong, the Svalbard Global Seed Vault may actually be the one thing that survives.

As of March 2010, there were roughly 500,000 different types of seeds in the vault. The goal is to store up to 1 million seed types, in hopes of covering the diversity of offerings the plant world has to share.

BONUS FACT

In Arizona, Pima County's public library system not only lends out books—it also "lends" out seeds. The "seed library" gives "borrowers" seeds to plant in their own gardens but asks that when the seeds grow into crops, the "borrowers" collect seeds and return an equal or greater amount to the library. The seed library notes that "there are no due dates or overdue fines" for the seeds.

THOU SHALT NOT DIE
THE ISLAND WHERE YOU AREN'T ALLOWED TO DIE

Throughout the ages, governments seemingly have tried to ban everything—other than death and taxes, so the saying goes. But the administrators of the Norwegian village called Longyearbyen in Svalbard are trying to change that, at least insofar as death is concerned.

Longyearbyen has a population of roughly 1,500 to 2,000 people. It is one of the northernmost places on Earth with any semblance of permanent residents. Located 78.22 degrees north, it is well within the Arctic Circle. Polar bears roam everywhere and, as one would guess, the temperatures never reach what most people would consider "warm." That point led to the ban on dying.

Before the ban, like anywhere else, people in Longyearbyen buried their dead. That makes sense—over time, the bodies of the deceased will decompose. Ashes to ashes, dust to dust, so to speak. But the words "over time" mean something different when you hit extremely low temperatures. And that can be dangerous—if not fatal—for the people who are still alive.

In 1917 a flu strain hit Longyearbyen, leading to the deaths of a number of residents, who were buried in the town cemetery. Thirteen years later, someone discovered that burying the dead in

Longyearbyen was a really, really bad idea. As the BBC reported, the bodies in the cemetery weren't decomposing. The cold earth had preserved the corpses and, as an unfortunate side effect, had also kept the influenza strain alive.

There is no reason to believe that anyone was infected by the resurrected influenza, but regardless, its discovery provided a warning to the town officials. Disturbing the ground in which a person was buried could trigger an outbreak of any communicable disease that afflicted the deceased at his or her death. Such a disease could spread rapidly throughout the island settlement. Realizing that Longyearbyen, quite isolated from the rest of the world, had no way of handling its dead—and the risk to the living—its leaders simply declared that dying was not permitted in the town.

Enforcement, of course, cannot be carried out via punitive action—"don't die, or else!" is a strange ultimatum, to say the least. Longyearbyen "prevents" people from dying in a few ways. The cemetery closed in 1930, accepting no future burials. The population is generally kept young, which makes sense regardless, given the climate. And though Longyearbyen doesn't by itself sound like a great retirement spot, the government drives the point home even more clearly—there's no elder care housing in the area.

If you fall deathly ill? The local authorities will airlift you to the nearest regional hospital, which is two hours away.

BONUS FACT

Longyearbyen is home to both the University Centre in Svalbard (UNIS) and a lot of polar bears as well. These beasts are savage and do not take kindly to people. So when a student, faculty member, or staff member enters UNIS, he or she goes right to class—riflery class, that is. Everyone at UNIS is trained in the use of a rifle to defend themselves from the polar bears.

NORWEGIAN WOOD
WHERE FIREWOOD IS SUPREMELY IMPORTANT

In many European (and American) cultures, it is traditional to light a fire on Christmas, and, specifically to use a "yule log"—a very large, hard log that can burn for hours on end. In 1966, WPIX, a television station based in New York, took the yule log to the airwaves. For a few hours on Christmas Eve, WPIX forwent advertising and their regular broadcasting schedule. Instead, WPIX went to Gracie Mansion (the official residence of the Mayor of New York) and filmed seventeen seconds of a yule log burning in the fireplace. A looped version recording became WPIX's Christmas Eve programming that year—and, incredibly, was a ratings success. Until 1989, WPIX made a point of broadcasting the commercial-free yule log for two to four hours every Christmas Eve.

This commitment to firewood is nothing compared to what happened in Norway.

In 2011, a Norwegian man named Lars Mytting wrote a book titled *Hel Ved*, or, in English, *Solid Wood: All About Chopping, Drying and Stacking Wood—and the Soul of Wood-Burning.* It sounds like any one of a billion titles you can find on Amazon, immediately making you wonder who would buy such a thing. With only about

5 million people in Norway altogether, it would not be surprising to hear that Mytting sold only five to ten copies of his book—if that.

In reality? He sold 150,000. His treatise on firewood was a bestseller.

Then it became a TV show. In February 2013, NRK, Norway's public broadcaster, explored turning the book into a series but opted instead to make it into a twelve-hour, same-day extravaganza. For four hours, the broadcast, according to *The New York Times*, aimed to "get to the core of Norwegian firewood culture"—1.2 million households in the country have either wood stoves or fireplaces—while "sawing," "splitting," "stacking," and "burning" firewood.

That, apparently, was the less interesting part of the program. For the next eight hours—eight hours!—NRK broadcast a fireplace, with logs burning. Unlike the WPIX yule log, though, this wasn't just a few minutes or seconds of film, looped. It was live television, not recorded, and of course, the fire had to be tended. During the eight hours of log burning, caretakers of the fire added and rearranged wood in the fireplace, keeping the blaze roaring throughout. Viewers were captivated, with an estimated one million people tuning in at some time during the broadcast. That's 20 percent of the country's population.

Sadly, not everyone was pleased with the show. Within the first few minutes of the Friday night broadcast, Mytting started receiving dozens of complaints via text message. The objection? Half wanted the wood stacked bark-up, the other half bark-down.

BONUS FACT

A twelve-hour show on firewood may seem strange to those of us not in Norway, but NRK has a history of curious programming. Gawker tells us that other specials popular in Norway, but unlikely to find a significant U.S. audience, include 134 hours of coverage of a cruise ship traveling up the Norwegian coast toward the Arctic and an eight-hour train ride from Oslo to Bergen.

A FESTIVUS FOR
THE PERUVIANS
THE CHRISTMAS DAY CELEBRATION THAT IS MORE
FIGHT CLUB *THAN* IT'S A WONDERFUL LIFE

During the ninth season of *Seinfeld*, George goes to his parents' house around Christmastime to celebrate a Costanza family tradition—the made-up holiday of Festivus. Festivus had a handful of traditions, including an aluminum pole instead of a Christmas tree, Festivus miracles (because what's a holiday without miracles?), dinner (of course), and two proper-noun events: the Feats of Strength and the Airing of Grievances.

The holiday, originally proposed by scriptwriter Dan O'Keefe, was based on O'Keefe's own experiences growing up. His family had an ad hoc celebration around Christmas as a way to relieve the tensions often associated with the Christmastime buildup. Both the Feats of Strength—a series of wrestling matches—and the Airing of Grievances aim to do just that, only in the fictional world of Jerry Seinfeld and his dysfunctional group of friends. Although many people have adopted Festivus as a tongue-in-cheek celebration since its first-time broadcast on *Seinfeld*, the holiday is fake.

Except, in a sense, in a small province in Peru.

The Peruvian province of Chumbivilcas, nestled in the Andes, is home to about 75,000 people. The population is rural and generally very poor; many speak the native language called Quechua, as the inhabitants of the area are still strongly linked to the culture of the Incan time period. Although Christianity has taken hold in many areas, traditional customs often have endured. One such custom is Takanakuy, which in Quechuan translates to "when the blood is boiling." On December 25—yes, Christmas Day—residents in the area dress up in traditional costumes and take to the street, dancing. Afterward, they gather in a field and beat each other up.

Two at a time—although often, things get out of hand—people with grudges engage in a bare-knuckled boxing match loosely refereed by a plainclothes member of the local authorities. As reported by Reuters, women and even children are allowed to step into the proverbial ring—the only limitation is that one can only square off against someone of the same gender and of similar age.

Both punching and kicking are allowed, but kicking someone when he or she is on the ground is forbidden and can result in the rule breaker finding him or herself on the wrong side of a whip. One need not have a grudge or rival in order to fight—many pugilists simply want to fight for the sake of fighting. It's a cultural event, after all, not just a chance for angry people to break others' noses.

And yes, participants often come out bloodied. But it is rare to hear reports of vengeance attacks afterward, perhaps because fighters know that they can demand a rematch a year later.

BONUS FACT

In 2000, Ben and Jerry's released an ice cream called "Festivus," after the *Seinfeld*-created holiday. According to *Mental Floss* magazine, it was a "base of brown sugar-cinnamon ice cream with gingerbread cookie chunks and a ginger caramel swirl." Unfortunately, you can't buy it for your own Festivus dinner—Ben and Jerry's discontinued the flavor and, barring a Festivus miracle, is not expected to bring it back.

ICE CREAM, YOU SCREAM
WHAT CAUSES ICE CREAM HEADACHES

"Sphenopalatine ganglioneuralgia" sounds like a terrible disease, and, certainly, it can be painful. But for most of us, sphenopalatine ganglioneuralgia is a punishment worthy of the crime—the crime of eating ice cream. Sphenopalatine ganglioneuralgia is the affliction better known as "brain freeze" or "ice cream headache," the stinging sensation one feels at the top/front of the head after eating too much ice cream too quickly.

Many of us have experienced it—one study in the *British Medical Journal* (yes, there's a study on ice cream headaches) suggests as many as one-third of the population has been so afflicted. Why does it happen? The most common explanation suggests that, in a sense, brain freezes are caused by our brains malfunctioning.

Your face has a nerve called the trigeminal nerve that contains three parts. One of the three parts carries sensory information from your forehead to your brain while another one does the same for the roof of your mouth. (The third one focuses on the lower mouth, but that's not relevant to conversations about ice cream headaches.) Eating ice cream causes the blood vessels in your face to contract quickly and, when the ice cream leaves your mouth, those same blood vessels get warm and dilate, or expand. If you eat ice cream too quickly, the blood vessels expand rapidly, and that's where the trigeminal nerve takes over. The part of the nerve in the roof of your mouth sends a signal to your brain, telling the brain that something's wrong.

The brain screws it up. This "mistake" is a phenomenon called "referred pain," in which the brain misplaces the source of the sensation. It's not very common, although it's also seen in heart attacks, during which the brain incorrectly places the pain in the shoulder instead of the chest. In the case of brain freeze, instead of "understanding" the signal for what it is—a change in temperature in your mouth—your brain instead thinks that the signal is coming from the forehead. The brain reacts by turning that signal into a migraine-like headache, although a short-lived one, thankfully.

Why this referred pain phenomenon occurs is unknown. But we do know that if you do not want to experience it, there's an easy solution: Slow down when you're eating a frosted treat.

BONUS FACT

The world's largest ice cream manufacturer and distributor is Unilever. They own Breyer's, Ben and Jerry's, Klondike, Good Humor, Popsicle, and . . . Slim Fast.

PUT ON A HAPPY FACE
THE COUNTER-INTUITIVE POWER OF SMILING

Our brains are very powerful, and many of the things we do happen at a subconscious level. For example, when we are happy, we smile, even without thinking about it. However, what if we did it consciously? What if we were feeling kind of down and smiled anyway?

As it turns out, that would be a great idea. Smiling can actually make you happy.

In July of 2012, *The Atlantic* reported on a study conducted by psychology researchers at the University of Kansas. The research team asked each of the 169 participants to make one of three preselected facial expressions—one showing no emotion or a neutral emotion; one with a standard smile; or a wide, high-cheek smile known as a Duchenne smile. The researchers then outfitted each person's mouth with chopsticks in order to keep the mandated facial expression in place during the rest of the experiment.

After the faces were set place, the participants performed a series of stressful activities that, along with keeping the chopsticks in place, required them to multitask. During this process, their heart rates were monitored and they were asked to keep tabs on their emotional states. The researchers compared their heart rates, emotional states, and facial expressions to one another and concluded that the bigger the smile, the more calm and relaxed the person was—even though the stressful activities were the same for each group.

This isn't the only study suggesting that smiling more can make you happier. A 2011 article in *Scientific American* reported on a study of twenty-five women, half of whom were undergoing Botox treatments. The dozen or so Botox users who were chemically unable to frown reported feeling less stressed and less anxious than the other group—even though their responses to other questions (such as how attractive they felt) were nearly identical to that of the control group. Similarly, according to HowStuffWorks.com, in 1989 a professor of psychology at the University of Michigan had test subjects make the long-vowel "e" sound, record their emotional states, then make the long-vowel "u" sound, and record their emotional states again. The subjects, by and large, were happier while making the smile-inducing "e" sound than the frown-inducing "u."

So the age-old advice, "Turn that frown upside down," may actually be worth taking. If you want to be a bit happier, try saying cheese.

BONUS FACT

Due to a severe winter in 1948, the mayor of Pocatello, Idaho, issued an ordinance requiring that townsfolk smile. (He probably was unaware that the idea was scientifically valid.) The ordinance went unrepealed but was forgotten for nearly forty years until, in 1987, a local reporter discovered it. The town revived the pseudo-law that year and declared the town the "U.S. Smile Capital." Pocatello instituted an annual "Smile Days" event. During the Smile Days, authorities make joking arrests of people who don't smile (and there's a town-wide party at the end of the week).

THE PERFECT CRIME SCENE
THE ONE PLACE IN THE UNITED STATES
WHERE THEY CAN'T GET YOU (MAYBE)

If you live in the United States, you're probably familiar with some of the basic rights guaranteed by the Bill of Rights—for example, freedom of speech, religion, the press; the right against self-incrimination; and the right for alleged criminals to be tried in front of a jury of their peers. But do you know what that last one means? It's more complicated than you'd think, and because of a strange legal wrinkle involving a very big national park, it may have created the perfect crime scene. At least, that's what law professor Brian Kalt of Michigan State University College of Law argues.

How does it work?

Let's say you, heaven forbid, are charged with a crime. The Constitution itself (Article III, Section 2 for those who wish to look it up) requires that the "trial shall be held in the State where the said crimes shall have been committed." Pretty straightforward. The Sixth Amendment requires that the jury must be "of the State and district wherein the crime shall have been committed." Again, pretty clear. The only confusing part, unless you're a lawyer, is probably the term "district."

The U.S. Federal Courts are divided into zones called "districts," which correlate almost perfectly with the states themselves. Connecticut has one district: the District of Connecticut. New York has four, using ordinal directions, e.g., "Southern District of New York," which includes Manhattan, the Bronx, and six counties in the state. Wyoming has one, as well, which includes the entire state. But for some reason, Congress decided to also include within the District of Wyoming the parts of Yellowstone National Park that are in Idaho and Montana. And that's where the perfect crime scene appears.

So that crime you're charged with? Imagine you committed it in the part of Yellowstone that is actually in Idaho. Where would your jury come from? It would have to be from the state (Idaho) *and* district (the District of Wyoming) in which the crime was committed. The only area that meets both requirements is that tiny portion of Yellowstone that is in Idaho. The population of that area?

Zero.

Good luck finding that jury.

BONUS FACT

During the 2008 U.S. presidential election, the four major party candidates, collectively, visited forty of the fifty states. Then-Senator Obama and Senator McCain's campaigns spent, in total, over $1 billion, according to Politico. Neither candidate visited Idaho or Wyoming that year, and Idaho received only $702 total in campaign advertising—$268 from Mr. Obama, $100 from Mr. McCain, and $334 from the Republican Party in support of McCain's campaign. For comparison's sake, the candidates spent nearly $2 million in neighboring Montana and more than $50 million in the battleground state of Ohio.

THE USUAL SUSPECTS
HOW THE NYPD FILLS POLICE LINEUPS

The 1995 movie *The Usual Suspects* won two Academy Awards—screenwriter Christopher McQuarrie won one for Best Original Screenplay and actor Kevin Spacey won one for Best Supporting Actor. The movie centers around five felons who are, inexplicably at the time, brought into the same lineup by the New York Police Department. The odd composition of the lineup strikes one of the five, Dean Keaton, as a telltale sign that the police have nothing on the quintet of suspects. At one point in the movie, Keaton and another felon, Michael McManus, discuss the peculiar mix:

> Keaton: This whole thing was a shakedown.
> McManus: What makes you say that?
> Keaton: How many times you been in a lineup? It's always you and four dummies. PD are paying homeless guys ten bucks a head half the time. And there's no way they'd line five felons in the same row. No way.

Keaton was right—kind of. The NYPD does pay about $10 per lineup stand-in. But they don't always pay homeless guys. Often, and especially in the Bronx, they pay Robert Watson.

Robert Watson is a nondescript man in his mid-forties who, according to a profile in *The New York Times* in October 2011, has a fondness for coconut-flavored booze. He's not a police officer but has an informal, working relationship with officers in his neighborhood. Watson got his "job" out of a stroke of luck—he was sitting around, minding his own business, when a police officer offered him a small stipend to sit in on a lineup. The officer then upped the ante, telling Watson that he could make a few extra bucks if he brought some friends along. Realizing that he could parlay this into a meaningful (albeit small) amount of income, Watson began playing headhunter for the PD and agent for the pseudo-actors who sit on stools waiting for witnesses.

For about fifteen years since, Watson has been on call, ready to provide the NYPD with lineup fillers—guys who aren't guilty of anything other than looking vaguely like the man accused of a crime. The people Watson provides sit, shoulder to shoulder, with the accused and other fillers, while the alleged victim or crime witness looks them over, deciding which (if any) is the person he or she believes committed the crime in question. If the accused is selected, that's good news for the prosecution; if not, that's excellent news for the defense.

Watson's informal relationship with the NYPD is his main source of income. He earns about $10 for each lineup filled, with the other monies going to the stand-ins themselves. (He sometimes sits in the lineup himself to make a bit extra.) On a good day, he'll fill four lineups; on a slow day, he'll come up empty. His annual earnings from his lineup filling business are, as one would expect, unreported, but probably hover around $10,000 a year. And—absent a public intoxication arrest—he stays out of trouble, lest he lose his marginally lucrative business.

According to the *Times*, he has a wide network of African Americans and Hispanics of both genders and can even provide men based on their facial hair or lack thereof. But as good at filling a lineup as Watson is, he's not perfect. When it comes to white people, Watson is of no help. He told the *Times* that "they call me for that, and I don't have that." Instead, Watson notes that the exchange from *The Usual Suspects* rings pretty true: "They go to the homeless shelter for white guys."

BONUS FACT

Another way to ID criminals, of course, is fingerprints. If you ever want to mask yours, consider getting a pet koala. Why? Because koala and human fingerprints are so similar that even experts have trouble telling them apart.

PRUNING UP
WHY OUR FINGERS WRINKLE WHEN WET

Spend enough time in a bathtub or a pool, and without fail your fingers will start to resemble raisins—pruned, wrinkled, etc. It's happened to all of us, many times. But why? What makes our fingers wrinkle when wet?

For a long time, the consensus involved absorption. As the theory goes, most things, when exposed to (or submerged in) water for a long period of time, tend to wilt or weaken. If that were to happen to our fingertips, we would probably lose their function temporarily if not permanently—and, of course, experience a huge amount of pain.

Wrinkling stops this. As noted by *Wired*, the puckered skin retains its cohesiveness, thereby avoiding that outcome. Your skin is not drying out; quite the opposite. It is actually absorbing a relatively large amount of water—*Wired* calls it a "tremendous" amount—while maintaining its function as the barrier between your other organs and the harsh environment around you.

Although this reasoning may be true, it may not be the only reason. One recent study reported on by *Discover* magazine concludes that pruney fingers have an evolutionary component—our fingers wrinkle so that we can grip things in wet conditions. Anecdotally, that makes a lot of sense—if our hands are submerged in water for a long period of time, there's a good chance the rest of our bodies are too. That means we may be in distress, unable to get ourselves out of the water and onto dry land. In theory, everything grabbable around us would also be wet, and therefore slick to the touch. Having smooth fingers would make it more difficult to grab hold of those would-be anchors, but when our fingers prune, so the theory goes, it is like having a personal set of rain treads.

A really interesting tidbit buttresses this theory: If your fingers' nerves are somehow severed from the rest of your nervous system (and therefore your brain), they no longer prune up in water. This almost certainly means that the pruning effect is triggered by the brain and is not simply related to absorption.

But other wrinkles (pardon the pun) remain. So far, we have not yet been able to determine whether pruney fingers do, in fact, help us grip wet things better. Also, there is demonstrable evidence of the first theory occurring—blood vessels contracting, skin absorbing water, etc.—which again suggests that there is a lot more going on there than we know.

BONUS FACT

Water can be used to check patients for brain damage, using something called the caloric reflex test. Typically, when cold water is inserted into a person's ear canal, his or her eyes will reflexively "look" toward the opposite ear. But when warm water is put in the person's ear, he or she will "look" toward the ear with the water in it. People with significant damage to the brain stem do not have the same reaction.

TEMPORARY BLINDNESS
THE ONE THING YOU CAN'T SEE IN THE MIRROR

Go to a mirror and look at either of your eyes. Then, while keeping your head still, look at the other one. As you do this, your gaze will change targets, as you are now looking at something different than before. But your eyes will not appear to move.

Now, go find a friend and repeat the experiment. Ask him or her to tell you if your eyes move as you glance from one eye to the other. Invariably, your friend will tell you that your eyes did indeed move—and obviously so. Switch roles and the illusion becomes obvious: Your friend, staring into the mirror, is moving his or her eyes—but unlike the rest of the world, sees no movement.

What's going on here? Our brains are protecting themselves from the fuzzy, blurry imagery we'd otherwise "see" as our eyes glance quickly from point to point. That movement—called a "saccade" (pronounced "sah-COD")—is simply too quick for our brains to deal with. So the brain, in effect, ignores what the eyes see, in a phenomenon called "saccadic masking." Instead of processing and recording the blurred image otherwise caused by the eye movement, the brain replaces that milliseconds-long moment with a still image of the second item your eyes look at. This image replacement can create an eerie effect if you quickly dart your eyes at an analog clock, causing the clock's second hand to appear momentarily frozen in time (known as the "stopped clock effect").

During these saccadic masking moments, we are, effectively, blind. According to some, these tiny moments of time lost down the memory hole add up to as much as thirty to forty-five minutes a day—leaving us temporarily blind for roughly 2 percent of our lives.

BONUS FACT

The eyes of most birds do not move. In order to keep their world from bouncing around as they move, these birds have developed the ability keep their heads in the same place, relative to the rest of the world, even if the rest of their bodies are in motion. That's why chickens, turkeys, pigeons, and other birds bob their heads as they walk—they're trying to keep their eyes parallel to the ground. It also helps them with depth perception. Turkeys, for example, have eyes on opposite sides of their heads, and therefore have no natural 3-D vision; the bobbing provides extra visual information so they can estimate relative distances. However, this does not mean they have worse vision than us humans. Turkeys can turn their necks much farther than people can, allowing them to see things a full 360 degrees around.

THE BIRD IS THE WORD
HOW THE TURKEY GOT ITS NAME

Every November, many American families gather around the table, feasting on a Thanksgiving meal—the centerpiece of which is a turkey. It's a celebration of many things but historically stems back to 1621, when European settlers ("Pilgrims," as American elementary school children will surely tell you) marked the harvest with a similar celebration.

Turkeys are indigenous to the United States and Mexico; in fact, Europeans only first came into contact with turkeys roughly 500 years ago, upon discovery of the New World. So how did the turkey (the bird) end up with the same name as Turkey (the country)? Let's follow that bird's history from the New World to the Old.

As far as we can tell, the first European explorers to discover (and eat) turkey were those in Hernán Cortés's expedition in Mexico in 1519. Spanish Conquistadors brought this new delicacy back to Europe and by 1524 it had reached England. The bird was domesticated in England within a decade, and by the turn of the century, its name—"turkey"—had entered the English language. Case in point: William Shakespeare used the term in *Twelfth Night*, believed to have been written in 1601 or 1602. The lack of context around his usage suggests that the term had widespread reach.

But the birds did not come directly from the New World to England; rather, they came via merchant ships from the eastern Mediterranean Sea. Those merchants were called "Turkey merchants" as much of the area was part of the Turkish Empire at the time. Purchasers of the birds back home in England thought the fowl came from the area, hence the name "Turkey birds" or, soon thereafter, "turkeys." To this day, we're simply carrying on the mistake of a few confused English-speaking Europeans.

But not all languages follow this misconception. Others, such as Hebrew, get the origin just as wrong, but in the other direction. The Hebrew term for turkey, transliterated as *tarnagol hodu*, literally translates to "chicken of India," furthering the Elizabethan-era myth that New World explorers had found a route to the Orient. This nomenclature for the bird is so widespread that it makes a mockery of the historical basis for the term "turkey" in English. Why? Because the Turkish word for turkey isn't "turkey." It's "hindi."

BONUS FACT

As for Turkey, the country? The story isn't as interesting. The word Turkey—actually, *Türkiye* in Turkish—can be broken up into two parts. "Türk" is a reference to people, potentially meaning "human beings" in an archaic version of the Turkish language. The "-iye" suffix most likely meant "land of."

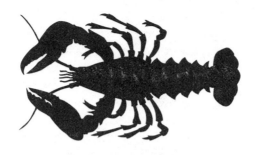

A PRINCELY MEAL
FIT FOR A PAUPER
THE DELICACY THAT WAS ONCE
RESERVED FOR THE POOR

At $10–15 a pound, lobster is priced too high to be anything other than a delicacy. Even if you bring home the crustacean alive and cook and prepare it yourself, it is going to be an expensive meal. So for most Americans, lobster is a menu item reserved for a special occasion. Weekly would be a lot; twice weekly is out of the question. Only in a dream, perhaps.

Or, if you were a rather poor worker in the early part of the nineteenth century, a nightmare.

Lobsters are very plentiful in coastal New England, particularly in Maine and Massachusetts. The Pilgrims likely dined on lobster at the first Thanksgiving and there are tales of two-foot high piles of lobsters simply washing up on the shores during that time period. And where things are plentiful, they're often cheap. Today, one can find high-quality lobster in Maine at about $5 a pound—much less than the going rate anywhere else. But from the 1600s through much of the 1800s, Maine and surrounding coastal areas were the *only* places one could reasonably find fresh-cooked lobster. As reported by the late David Foster Wallace in the similarly deceased *Gourmet* magazine, before we had the infrastructure and equipment required to ship live lobsters around the country (and later the world), the crustaceans were killed before they were cooked, just like almost any other animal. Precooked lobster meat in hermetically sealed cans doesn't taste very good; Wallace noted that the protein-rich meat was used as "chewable fuel," and not as the culinary draw we think of it as today.

Massive quantities of cheap food that doesn't taste very good . . . that's not a recipe for thrilling dinner guests. It is, however, a solution to other problems—such as, how do you feed prison inmates or indentured servants? That's exactly where the lobster meat ended up. Wallace says that some states had rules insisting that inmates not be fed canned lobster meat more than once per week, and other sources note that indentured servants often demanded that their contracts limit the lobster meals to no more than twice weekly.

Once lobsters could be transported, alive, over long distances, the Maine lobster canneries began closing up shop. In the 1880s, lobster started to become a much-sought-after entree in Boston and New York, and over the next few decades, that custom spread across the country. By World War II, lobster was a high-priced treat—officially. Most foods were subject to wartime rationing, but not lobster because of its designation as a delicacy.

BONUS FACT

Generally speaking, expensive versions of a food item taste better than their cheaper counterparts. (After all, that's why they're more expensive.) Lobster—the cooked-live variety—is the exact opposite. Lobster quality is rated based on the hardness of its shell, as lobsters that have recently shed their old shells (and are growing new ones) typically have the sweetest and most desirable meat. Unfortunately, they also have the least amount of meat and are the hardest to transport, because their shells are so new. So these lobsters are kept local to New England and are only served in places where lobster is relatively common. Lower-quality lobsters, with harder shells and with more meat, are shipped around the world, and are the only lobsters offered to the captive markets. Because of this a lobster in Europe will almost certainly be of lower quality than one in Maine, but will cost as much as ten times the price.

THE GREATEST THING SINCE 1928

THE HISTORY OF SLICED BREAD (AND WHY IT WAS ONCE BANNED)

The Internet. The automobile. Toilet paper. All these have been heralded as the greatest things since sliced bread. Which means that sliced bread, itself, has to be a pretty amazing thing.

Turns out, it is. But in order for us to collectively learn that lesson, the American government had to ban it.

Sliced bread—machine-sliced, that is—was almost invented in 1912, when a man named Otto Fredrick Rohwedder came up with a prototype and blueprints for an automated bread-slicing machine but lost his work to a fire. Undeterred, Rohwedder rebuilt the machine held in his mind's eye. In 1928, he had a machine up and running, and by July of that year, sliced bread was being machine-produced for the masses. The marketing behind the product set the stage for the neologism used today, as Rohwedder's bread was advertised as "the greatest forward step in the baking industry since bread was wrapped." By 1930, Wonder Bread switched to a sliced-bread product, selling machine-sliced bread nationwide for the first time.

Sliced bread made bread consumption increase, as expected. But when World War II rationing came to the forefront of the

American economic war effort, Food Administrator Claude Wickard targeted the greatest invention of the century (so to speak). Hoping to reduce the amount of wax paper used in general—because, Wickard presumed for some reason that sliced bread required more wax paper than its unsliced counterpart—and also hoping to reduce bread prices, Wickard banned the sale of sliced bread domestically, effective January 18, 1943. This was immediately met with protestations from housewives arguing that their household efficiencies were crippled by a short-sighted ban. Because, after all, sliced bread was the greatest thing in recent memory.

Local politicians took the matter into their own hands. New York City mayor Fiorello LaGuardia noted that bakeries could use their own bread-slicing machines, selling the freshly baked (and sliced) product direct to their customers. But the Food Distribution Association put the kibosh on that several days later, requiring the cessation of any commercial bread slicing, in order to protect those bakeries that either did not have bread-slicing machinery or wished to do their all for the country's war efforts.

In any event, the ban was short lived. On March 8, sliced bread was once again allowed in the United States, its greatness preserved for generations present and future.

BONUS FACT

Toilet paper is not the greatest thing since sliced bread—it can't be, because toilet paper predates sliced bread by more than fifty years. Commercial toilet paper was invented in 1857 by a New Yorker named Joseph Gayetty, who sold packs of 500 sheets (each containing a watermark with his name) for fifty cents. Its marketing language called the product "the greatest necessity of the age," so perhaps, sliced bread is the greatest thing since toilet paper.

COLOR BY NUMBER
WHAT THE TAGS ON YOUR LOAVES OF BREAD MEAN

Go to any grocery store bread aisle and you'll find—one hopes!—bread. Most of the bread does not just sit on the racks as is; typically, the loaves are wrapped in bags, held shut with a twist tie or a plastic tag. And you may notice that many of those ties and tags are colored—blue, orange, green, or a litany of other hues. In many cases, the colors vary even within the same brand; the shelf of Wonder Bread may have tags of five different colors.

Laziness? Rampant colorblindness in the factory? Or maybe bread makers just don't care? Nope. For some, it's a quality assurance tactic.

For more than a decade, Internet folklore claimed that the tags were quick visual clues that indicated the day of the week that the bread was baked. The urban legend held that stock clerks could easily identify loaves that were no longer fresh by looking for tags of a certain color. This would save a lot of time, as manually looking at expiration dates is labor intensive. In theory, so the legend goes, bread makers used these ties to make the supermarkets' jobs easier, and thus making it much less likely that a customer would have a bad experience.

According to urban legend fact-checker Snopes, this piece of Internet folklore is—a rarity!—mostly true. Many bread manufacturers use different color tags each day, in order to help ensure that what reaches the end consumer is of high quality.

But there is no need to try and crack the code—and, in fact, it probably isn't possible for the average consumer, because there isn't only one system. Although news reports about the bread tags (and even more often, the e-mails forwarded around) suggest that savvy consumers can avoid getting a stale loaf simply paying attention to the tags, that isn't the case. In general, the color system is intended for the supermarkets, whose employees should be removing the old bread before it goes stale. Similarly, the color-coding system is not standardized across all brands; each manufacturer can choose to adopt its own system, if it adopts one at all. For example, when a CBS San Francisco reporter followed up on the Snopes report, she found that at least one company simply printed the expiration date on their (always light blue) tags. As a consumer, therefore, it is always better to check the sell-by date.

If you want to have an extra level of comfort that your bread is fresh, you can follow Snopes' advice: "Contact the manufacturer of your favorite brand and ask" about their color-coding system.

BONUS FACT

The color orange is named after the fruit, not the other way around. The fruit's original name in English was probably something closer to its current name in Spanish, *naranja*. Over time, the first letter "n" disappeared from the word, most likely because when combined with the definite article—for example, "*una naranja*" in Spanish—the sounds run together. The "au" sound dominated the start of the word, finally turning into "orange."

ORANGE GOES GREEN
WHY YOUR MORNING ORANGE JUICE MAY BE AT RISK

Oranges are orange. Some things in life are just that simple. But that fact is becoming increasingly untrue, and there may not be much we can do about it. The bacteria are winning, and orange oranges are their victims.

In 2006, some Florida citrus growers detected bacteria called Las (*Candidatus Liberibacter asiaticus*, for the armchair biologists) on their trees. Las causes a disease originally discovered in Asia called Huanglongbing, or HLB. Once a tree is infected with HLB, it cannot be cured and, according to the U.S. Department of Agriculture, dies within five to ten years. (A healthy orange tree can live for as long as a century.) Oranges from trees infected with HLB do not ripen the same way those from healthy trees do and end up misshapen. Further, most of them aren't entirely orange. They're mostly green.

A certain type of insect carries the disease, so even if farmers cut down infected plants, Las will still find a way to spread. According to *Scientific American*, the citrus industry invests about $16 million annually in the fight against the bugs, bacteria, and disease, but for the moment, it does not have a solution. The insect itself—called the Asian citrus psyllid—is a difficult target, because it is incredibly tiny; the USDA notes that it is "no bigger than the head of a pin."

Although this is bad news for citrus growers, it isn't a nightmare scenario for lovers of orange juice—at least not yet. The green, misshapen, and diseased fruits are perfectly safe to eat. Their chemical makeup is a bit different than typical oranges and they taste slightly more bitter because of that. However, as *Smithsonian* magazine notes, the taste difference is too subtle for the typical person to notice. Mixing the juice of the "bad" fruit with juice from uninfected oranges masks the bitter taste enough to make it almost entirely undetectable, so there is no immediate risk to the OJ market, so long as enough healthy citrus trees exist.

More good news is that by themselves the Asian citrus psyllids cannot travel long distances, so the disease is not able to spread too far—unless people end up assisting its spread. And that is exactly what is happening. The USDA has set up a website, www.SaveOur Citrus.org, that specifically advises people to "reduce the spread of citrus diseases by not moving your homegrown citrus fruit or plants across state lines." Video and radio ads echo that request. For the sake of OJ drinkers everywhere, it hopes people will heed that call.

BONUS FACT

Brush your teeth and then drink some OJ, and you're in for a rude surprise—the juice tastes downright awful. What causes that? Most toothpastes contain a compound called sodium laureth sulfate, which causes the foaming action when you brush. But it also blocks your tongue from being able to detect sweetness. So when you drink the juice, you're unable to taste the sweet aspects; instead, you only sense the bitter/sour parts.

GONE BANANAS
YOU AREN'T EATING YOUR GRANDPARENTS' BANANAS

Seedless. Nutritious. Portable. Tasty. Yellow. You pretty much know what you're going to get with a banana. And you should get it before it's gone.

Bananas—or more accurately, the Cavendish, a specific type of banana that most of us consider to be *the* banana—are, if nothing else, an incredibly consistent fruit. There's a reason for that. All Cavendish bananas are clones and therefore genetically identical to every other Cavendish out there. (It's not uncommon for fruits to be cloned. Navel oranges are also clones, for example.) But being clones has a big downside—if there's a disease that affects one Cavendish, it affects all Cavendish.

Which is why the bananas most people eat—and we eat a lot of them, more than twenty-five pounds of bananas per American each year (that's the most of any fresh fruit!)—aren't the same bananas that were eaten fifty years ago. Prior to 1960, the standard commercial banana type was the Gros Michel (a.k.a. "Big Mike"), a larger banana type that, by many accounts, was also tastier. But the Gros Michel was susceptible to Panama disease, caused by a fungus that attacks the roots of banana plants. Panama disease spread rapidly through major banana plantations, crippling businesses and making Gros Michel cultivation commercially impossible. After billions of dollars of research and development, the Cavendish—which is genetically resistant to Panama disease—became the world's top banana.

Could the Cavendish go the way of the dodo and the Gros Michel? Absolutely. A relatively new strain of Panama disease, Tropical Race 4 ("TR4"), can destroy Cavendish crops, and the only known way to stop it is genetic resistance, which the Cavendish (being a clone) won't ever develop. TR4 has already attacked banana plantations in Australia, Taiwan, Malaysia, Indonesia, and has spread to Southeast Asia. According to *Popular Science*, experts believe that it is only a matter of time, perhaps decades, before TR4 sends the Cavendish down the same path as Big Mike. But there's a very good chance that it could be longer. Plantation owners learned their lessons from the Gros Michel banana Apocalypse and take extreme measures to prevent this from repeating; there are even reports of plantations burning down entire fields due to a slight Panama disease infection, hoping to stop its spread.

BONUS FACT

Bananas are radioactive. Specifically, the potassium they contain is actually a rare radioactive isotope. The radiation is at low enough levels that it is not very dangerous: Eating 2,000 bananas will have the same toll on your lifespan as smoking one and a half cigarettes, according to Wikipedia. That said, the amount of radioactivity is real and measurable, so much so that bananas have been known to set off false alarms at U.S. ports where officials are looking for smugglers of nuclear materials.

RADIOACTIVE RED
THE RADIOACTIVE PLATES IN YOUR KITCHEN

In the 1930s, a certain brand of dinnerware was all the rage—Fiestaware. Unlike most dishes, which were mostly white, Fiesta's came in a variety of colors—blue, ivory, green, yellow, and orangeish-red. The popularity of these dishes was beyond comparison (for dishes, at least)—even famed artist Andy Warhol was among Fiesta's legions of fans. Two of the colors were also difficult to copy. Fiesta's red and, to a lesser extent, ivory dinnerware required a special, expensive ingredient in order to make the colored glaze.

That ingredient? Uranium. Fiestaware was radioactive.

Fiesta made its way into American homes in the mid-1930s, advertised as the first solid-color dinnerware available. (Some smaller brands made similar offerings but nothing on a national scale.) To obtain the red glaze, Fiesta used uranium oxide, which did the job but, of course, has the unfortunate side effect of needing uranium. In 1944, the presence of uranium in the dishes led its manufacturer, the Homer Laughlin China Company, to eventually pull them off the shelves.

But not for health reasons—the potential for harm caused by the radioactive dinnerware is still debatable. The red dishes disappeared from shelves due to national security needs. That year, the United States, under the Manhattan Project, was trying to develop an atomic bomb and needed uranium. The government seized any and all uranium it could find, including that owned by Homer Laughlin. The company pulled the red offering from its product line later that year.

In 1959, the red Fiestaware made a comeback, this time using less radioactive depleted uranium instead of natural uranium. As for the vintage, much more radioactive stuff? It may be okay to keep as a collectible, but the EPA lists it as emitting "elevated levels" of radiation—so collector (and certainly, everyday diner) beware.

BONUS FACT

Red M&Ms aren't radioactive, but they, too, have a story. In 1976, the popular red food coloring amaranth was pulled from shelves due to fears of it being carcinogenic. Although red M&Ms did not use amaranth, Mars, Inc. nevertheless removed red M&Ms from the packaging to avoid confusion and fear. In 1987, red came back, using a coloring called Allura Red AC, which may cause hyperactive behavior in younger children. (The operative word there, though, is "may." It probably doesn't.) Because of this, in some areas—most notably, parts of Europe—red M&Ms are colored with cochineal dye. Cochineal dye is produced by a certain type of insect (the cochineal, from which the dye's name comes), and to extract it, the insect is reduced to a powder and boiled.

BULL'S EYES
DO BULLS REALLY HATE THE COLOR RED? (NOPE.)

Modern Spanish-style bullfighting dates back to 1726. That year, a *matador de toros*—literally, "killer of bulls"—named Francisco Romero revolutionized the tradition. He took on the bulls on foot, unlike his predecessors who had battled the animals while on horseback. More importantly, Romero introduced some new equipment into the battlefield—a sword called an *estoque*, and a cape known as a *muleta*. As we all know, the *muleta* is, traditionally, red.

The bulls, on the other hand, have no idea what color it is.

For nearly 300 years, matadors have mimicked Romero's costume. At some time during the past three centuries, the red cape became the subject of a myth: When bulls see the color red, they become irate and charge at it. The myth is so widespread that it even permeated children's cartoons: The protagonist finds himself in the arena with a bull and (often accidentally) shows something red to the creature. This, in the cartoons, enrages the bull, putting the cartoon character's life in peril.

But in reality, that's not the case. People have trichromatic vision—we have three different color receptors in our eyes. Bulls have dichromatic vision; that is, they only have two color receptors. We can look at the *muleta* and determine that it is red. Bulls, on the other hand, can't discern between colors well enough to recognize red.

On the August 22, 2007 episode of *Mythbusters*, the cast put this to the test. First, they put out red, white, and blue flags; the bull charged at each one, without any noticeably extra ire directed toward the red one. Next, the Mythbusters dressed three dummies as matadors, one in each of the three colors. The red matador met the bull's horns last. Finally—most conclusively, too—one of the Mythbusters dressed in all red, but stayed as still as possible while two professionals, wearing blue or white, respectively, danced around the bullring. The bull ignored the red-clad Mythbuster and instead chased the dancing cowboys.

Most likely, bulls are attracted to the *muletas* due to the movements the matadors make with them, and not because of their color. For the most part, the red *muletas* are still used out of respect for tradition, but there's a second reason. Although the bulls can't tell that the matadors' capes are red, the audience certainly can. When the bull wins, the *muleta*'s color masks the matador's blood. With well over 500 matadors dying in bullfights since Romero reinvented bullfighting, that's probably a good thing.

BONUS FACT

Bulls (and many other animals) only have two color receptors, but the fact that humans have three is not that amazing. Butterflies have five, and according to *Nature*, one species, the mantis shrimp, has at least ten—and maybe more.

BLOOD FALLS
THE ALIEN-LIKE LIFE FORMS TRAPPED IN ANTARCTICA

Travel south from New Zealand and you'll eventually hit Antarctica. Continue inward on the southern continent and you'll end up passing through a thirty-four-mile long Antarctic glacier known as the Taylor Glacier, named after Griffith Taylor, a geologist and Australian explorer who was one of the first people to lead exploratory expeditions of the area. Next to the Taylor Glacier is Lake Bonney, a saltwater lake trapped under an ice shelf ten to fifteen feet thick. Oozing slowly from underneath Taylor Glacier and onto Lake Bonney's ice cover is a five-story-high frozen waterfall.

The water comes out blood red. And that isn't even the most interesting part of what is now called Blood Falls.

Griffith Taylor discovered Blood Falls in 1911. At the time, Taylor and others believed that there was some sort of algae alive in the glacier, creating the dark-red tint in the ice. As it turned out, this isn't the case.

Buried well below Taylor Glacier—we're not entirely sure how far below—is a prehistoric lake, which has been trapped there, undisturbed, for an estimated 1.5 to 2 million years. The lake is entirely cut off from the rest of the Earth's outer environment. It receives no sunlight. It has no oxygen. It has very high levels of saline (it's a saltwater lake), sulfur, chloride, and iron. (The iron oxides cause the seepage at Blood Falls to turn red.) As one would expect, the temperature of the water hits extremely low levels; the high amount of salt is the only thing keeping the water from easily freezing.

What may seem like an inhospitable environment, though, is anything but. There's something living in this subglacial lake, and given the lake's seclusion, the life forms have been there for millennia. They aren't the Loch Ness Monster or the Yeti, but according to *Science* magazine, multiple species of microbes live in the lake—at least a dozen and perhaps twice that. They've somehow survived without oxygen or any known way of producing it. The leading theory suggests that the microbes somehow use the sulfate and iron instead, but because no other known life form on Earth does this, we don't understand how.

However, the microbes are there, which is particularly fascinating because by all rights they shouldn't be. They're often cited as examples as to why we can't rule out life on places such as Mars or Jupiter's ice-covered moon Europa; if something could survive beneath Taylor Glacier for an epoch, there could be something alive out there too.

BONUS FACT

On April 20, 1967, NASA landed a probe called the *Surveyor 3* on the surface of the moon. Two and a half years later, the *Apollo 12* team recovered *Surveyor 3* from the moon's surface. According to NASA, microbes from Earth—which were likely present when *Surveyor 3* launched—were found present when the *Apollo 12* team returned the probe to Earth. Although some people question the validity of the discovery, if it's true, the microbes (bacteria called *Streptococcus mitis*) survived exposed space travel and, for that matter, a lot of time on the moon. Since the discovery of the *Surveyor 3* microbes, NASA has implemented a more thorough sweep for microbes for all spaceflights in order to avoid accidentally introducing life into the universe outside of Earth's atmosphere.

LEAVING MARKS
THE UNSOLVED, MYSTERIOUS DEATH
AT THE BOTTOM OF THE EARTH

Australian-born Rodney Marks died on May 12, 2000, not far from the geographic South Pole. He had been working as an astrophysicist at the Amundsen-Scott South Pole Station, a research facility run by the U.S. government via the National Science Foundation (NSF). The NSF originally concluded that Marks died due to natural causes. Six months later, and for more than a decade since, that finding has looked increasingly dubious. However, in part because of the quirks of how Antarctica is legally organized, we may never know what happened.

Marks, an accomplished researcher, was at the South Pole working on a telescope. He suffered from Tourette's syndrome and tended to go on drinking binges in part to mask the symptoms of the condition. (Yes, there are bars in Antarctica. Several, in fact.) He was engaged to be married, and his fiancée, a woman named Sonja Walter, had taken a job at the South Pole to be with him. But on May 11, 2000, he began to feel very ill. He saw the doctor three times in the next day and a half, but it was all for naught, as no reason for his illness could be found.. About thirty-six hours after taking ill, Marks was dead.

In most cases, the police would be called in. But Antarctica isn't owned by a single country, and although there are international treaties discussing rights and responsibilities to parts of it, many of the jurisdictional claims are unresolved. New Zealand makes a territorial claim on the area around the South Pole in which much of the U.S. presence is located. The United States does not recognize this claim, but it hasn't objected when New Zealand applied New Zealand law to New Zealanders working for the United States in that area. Similarly, New Zealand has never objected to U.S. authorities investigating crimes committed in the area.

Six months after his death, Marks's body was shipped to New Zealand for an autopsy (with the blessing of the United States). The coroner determined that Marks died from methanol poisoning and referred the case to the New Zealand police for further investigation. Methanol poisoning occurs, typically, when a person drinks antifreeze or Sterno in hopes of getting an effect similar to that of alcohol (that is, to get drunk), but the New Zealand authorities noted that Marks had access to plenty of alcohol and wouldn't likely accidentally drink those things. Further, investigators openly doubted that Marks would have committed suicide—after all, he repeatedly sought medical treatment.

As chief investigator Detective Senior Sergeant Grant Wormald told the press, that is as far as the police work got. When New Zealand authorities tried to get information from potential witnesses or from the relevant organizations' files, no one was willing to speak and denied that New Zealand had jurisdiction over the matter. When the U.S. Department of Justice stepped in to help, the people and organizations involved claimed the United States did not have jurisdiction either. The investigation ground to a halt in 2008, and Marks's father told the *New Zealand Herald* that it was unlikely that more details would come to light.

To date, the mystery remains unsolved.

BONUS FACT

Each year, researchers place a marker in the glacial ice at the site of the geographic South Pole. Because the ice shifts over time, the marker is at a different location within the ice each year. In theory, there should be a lot of markers seemingly scattered across the Antarctic floor. However, that's not the case—the markers are inside, on display in a museum-like environment. Well, most of the markers are on display, at least. According to a 2003 report in the *Antarctic Sun* (a newsletter from those stationed on the icy continent), at least one of the markers was missing and presumed stolen by the time the decision to bring them inside was made. There are no known suspects.

NO MAN'S LAND
THE ONE PIECE OF LAND NO COUNTRY OWNS

Roughly 30 percent of the Earth's surface is land. And where there is land, there is a nation (or multiple nations) ready to claim it as its own. In fact, some of the world's strangest disputes have been over pieces of land so small as to inspire bemused disbelief. Outside of Antarctica, almost every square foot of land is claimed by at least one nation.

Except for an 800-square-mile piece of land call Bir Tawil.

Bir Tawil sits between Egypt and Sudan. Neither country wants the land; in fact, each would be happy if the other took it. The area is landlocked and barren. The terrain is dry and mountainous and no one lives there permanently. A century ago, a tribe of nomads used the area as grazing lands, but that has long since changed. "Bir Tawil" translates to "deep water well," a name given to the area decades ago due to the presence of a well in the region (and literally nothing else), but even that well is long gone.

But Bir Tawil's general worthlessness is not why neither country wants it. Rather, the nations don't want it because it would preclude them from claiming the Hala'ib Triangle, which sits to Bir Tawil's northeast. Much larger and with fertile soil bordering the Red Sea, the triangle is claimed by both Egypt and Sudan.

The dispute over the Hala'ib Triangle dates back to two edicts, one from 1899 and another in 1902. In 1899, the United Kingdom (which controlled the area) drew the northern border of Sudan at the 22nd Parallel, a straight line stretching east to the Red Sea. Under these borders, Egypt would control the Hala'ib Triangle and Bir Tawil (as these regions are called today) would fall to Sudan. But these borders had a small flaw. A group of people living in the triangle were both geographically and culturally closer to the Sudanese capital of Khartoum. It made little sense for these people to be Egyptians when they could so easily be Sudanese. To fix this, in 1902, the UK decided to draw a jagged "administrative boundary" which placed the Hala'ib Triangle under the administration of Sudan. However, for some reason, instead of starting this boundary at the 22nd Parallel and moving northeast, the British began the line south of the Parallel. In doing so, it carved out a small divot, now known as Bir Tawil, to be administered by Egypt.

Today, Egypt recognizes the straight-line 1899 border. Sudan claims the jagged 1902 border. As a result, no one wants Bir Tawil, making it the only place, other than Antarctica, unclaimed by any nation.

BONUS FACT

In October 2006, the United States passed the "Secure Fence Act of 2006," which endeavored to build a border fence across its southwest border with Mexico. The fence, however, does not track the border exactly because a treaty between the United States and Mexico prevents development in the Rio Grande floodplain in Texas. According to Yahoo News, the Americans built some sections of the fence about a mile north of the border, placing some Texans, still technically in the United States, on the Mexican side of the fence.

GARBAGE CITY
HOW CAIRO'S GARBAGE CREATED A LOCAL ECONOMY

Cairo, the capital of Egypt, is one of the largest urban areas in the world, with over 6.5 million residents in the city itself and roughly 18 million in the greater metro area. It is like most cosmopolitan cities, except for one interesting difference: garbage.

Cairo's municipal waste system—which handles about 9,000 tons of garbage a day—is not much of a system at all. It is, at best, an informal undertaking. The city's municipal garbage needs are driven by a subset of the population known as the Zabbaleen (literally, "garbage people" in Egyptian Arabic), a group of mostly Coptic Christians numbering around 60–70,000 who have been the city's *de facto* garbage collectors for decades. They live in a half-dozen or so communities in the outskirts of Cairo, collecting trash and refuse from virtually every street corner in the city.

Where the garbage ends up is, perhaps, the real story. The Zabbaleen collect the trash in a village named Manshiyat Naser, a slum, with stores and dwellings, avenues and roads, but without a sewer system, running water, or electricity. The streets of the village are strewn with trash. For this, the village has earned the moniker "Garbage City."

But this isn't necessarily a bad thing. At Manshiyat Naser, the Zabbaleen work their magic with the refuse of others, sorting through tons and tons of it for items that can be reused or recycled—or, in the case of food, fed to pigs. (When the swine flu made its way around the world, the Egyptian government ended that practice.) Families specialize in types of garbage and thereby are able to better pick out treasure from, well, actual trash. The results are apparently spectacular—according to a 2010 documentary about the Zabbaleen and Manshiyat Naser, as much as 80 percent of the garbage can be repurposed. For comparison's sake, most recycling methods recover only about a quarter of items thrown away.

The Zabbaleen's future, however, is up in the air. The culling of pigs due to the swine flu scare wreaked havoc on their economy. Combined with Egypt and Cairo's prerevolutionary desire to become more modern and turn garbage collection into a municipal service, the Zabbaleen's role in Cairo's garbage economy may be on the wane.

BONUS FACT

According to Dr. Robin Nagle, anthropologist-in-residence at the New York City Department of Sanitation (it's a part-time job), "Sanitation workers are at greater risk of on-the-job injury and on-the-job fatality than police officers or fire fighters."

THE TRASH COLLECTORS
WHY SWEDEN IMPORTS TRASH

According to *National Geographic*, about 55 percent of trash generated by Americans ends up in landfills. About a third is recycled and the remaining 12.5 percent or so gets incinerated. Lowering that first number seems like a good idea for many reasons—landfills take up space, create methane gas, and can taint groundwater supplies. Garbage isn't only a problem for the United States; other countries' populations also create trash by the barrelful each week.

But Sweden has a totally different garbage problem. They simply don't have enough of it.

According to a story on NPR, only about 4 percent of Swedish refuse finds its way to the landfill. That's because, in large part, Sweden incinerates a huge percentage of its trash. In doing so, the country captures a huge amount of energy. Many parts of Sweden use something called "district heating," a centralized system in which (in this case) garbage is burned to heat water, and that heated water is then piped to residential and commercial buildings to provide heat. By burning garbage, Sweden is able to produce 20 percent of its district heating needs, as well as electricity to about 250,000 homes. Almost everything is used—even medical waste. In fact, Sweden is so good at turning trash into energy that, as Public Radio International reported in the summer of 2012, the country had more need for electricity than trash available. Put bluntly, they needed more garbage.

The good thing about needing garbage? There's usually a lot available, and others are more than willing to get rid of it. Not only that, but people—governments, in this case—will pay you to take it off their hands. So when Sweden went looking for more garbage, they found that neighboring Norway was not only willing to send some garbage Sweden's way, but they also provided a bit of extra revenue to the Swedes.

For now. Sweden may have to look elsewhere soon (they already are, with Italy, Romania, Bulgaria, and others in their sights). Many other nations, especially those in Northern Europe, are investing in similar processes and systems—and they'll need their trash. In April 2013, *The New York Times* reported that Oslo, Norway's capital, had itself become a net importer of garbage— the city was able to heat "roughly half the city and most of its schools" by burning garbage. However, like Sweden, it ran out of trash and is now importing it from neighboring areas.

BONUS FACT

The official Twitter account of Sweden (@sweden, naturally) is run by a different Swedish citizen each week.

PORK PROJECT
CHINA'S NATIONAL PORK RESERVES

As we said, governments often stockpile items (garbage, as noted) for strategic, often economic purposes. The United States has a Strategic Petroleum Reserve (SPR), for example—a stockpile of oil, worth, as of December 21, 2012, well over $60 billion. The purpose of the SPR is to prevent foreign entities from causing economic harm to the United States by refusing to sell petroleum to America. The SPR was formed after the 1973 oil crisis and now has nearly 700 million barrels of oil. That's enough to mitigate potential embargoes for months. Given American (and international) reliance on petroleum, the SPR makes a lot of sense.

America isn't alone here. Most other developed nations also have strategic oil reserves; China, for example, has 100 million barrels under lock and key, with plans for another 375 million to be added. Nothing out of the ordinary.

But the Chinese don't stop there. They also have a strategic reserve of something else: pork.

Pork has become a staple in China. According to the Earth Policy Institute, China consumed only 8 million tons of meat in 1978—that's about one-third of what Americans consumed in the same year. But by 2010, China consumed 71 million tons, double the United States's amount. About three-quarters of that was pork. Given the growing demand for pork products, keeping prices stable became a problem. So in 2007, per *The New York Times*, the Chinese government created a "national pork reserve." When prices spike, China is able to add to the pork supply, nudging the price back down.

Kind of. Unfortunately, unlike petroleum, frozen pork has a relatively short shelf life—the *Times* puts it at four months—and live pigs have an ongoing upkeep cost. In 2011, when China considered opening the pork reserves' doors in order to keep up with demand, the 200,000 metric tons it had available were not enough to make a meaningful difference in price.

On the other hand, the pork reserve has another use—and an easily accomplished one at that. When prices fall, the government can simply purchase more, stocking up while simultaneously inflating prices. This is especially important when corn prices stay high, as pigs are fed cornmeal and if the price of feeding them outweighs their value, the supply of pork can, somewhat paradoxically, crash suddenly. For this reason, in the spring of 2013, the Chinese government began buying up surplus pork, specifically in an effort to rally the price.

BONUS FACT

Almost all of Saudi Arabia's radio and television programs are broadcast by a government entity known as BSKSA. BSKSA censors programs to make sure that their content is consistent with the tenets of Islam, and, therefore, BSKSA disallows references to pork.

THE GREAT SYRUP CAPER
THAT TIME WHEN A WHOLE LOT OF MAPLE SYRUP WAS STOLEN FROM CANADA'S MAPLE SYRUP RESERVES

Another odd strategic reserve? Canada has one for maple syrup. Or, more accurately, in 2000 a group of maple syrup producers in Quebec created one, in hopes of keeping maple syrup prices constant from year to year. The length of "tapping season"—*The New York Times* defined it as "the narrow window of freezing nights and daytime temperatures over 40 degrees needed to convert starch to sugar and get sap flowing"—is fickle, dependent on the weather. Some seasons provide for a lot of maple syrup, which is bad for producers because high supplies force the price down. Other seasons provide for very little maple syrup, which is bad for some producers because they don't have the volumes needed to keep business going profitably. The good news is that unopened maple syrup has a shelf life of years and doesn't require any refrigeration. So "strategic reserves" help stabilize prices.

Until they go missing.

The market for maple syrup in Quebec is tightly controlled. You can't simply plant a sugar maple and tap your tree; you must either acquire land from someone who has a license, or request one from the Federation of Quebec Maple Syrup Producers (really). But the latter route is a slow, cumbersome process—as of early 2013, there were well over 1,000 names on that waiting list. The Federation monitors the output of licensees, in hopes of preventing them from stashing some syrup on the side and selling it directly. Yes, there's a black market for maple syrup. And its motive is not just profit: Plenty of people out there ideologically frown on the Federation's objectives and act against it.

In the summer of 2012, during what *The Wall Street Journal* called a "routine inventory check" at a maple syrup storage facility, an inspector found something wrong. Barrels that should have contained a million pounds of syrup were in fact filled with water. In total, 10 million pounds of syrup—valued at about $3 U.S. per pound—were gone. Officials did not think that the theft would harm the global supply of maple syrup (Quebec produces about three-quarters of it); there was enough supply to go around. But of course, the thieves would have to sell the stolen syrup (a person can only eat so many pancakes), which isn't good for suppliers who are now competing against their own, stolen product.

Eventually, two-thirds of the stolen syrup was recovered. The alleged culprit mastermind was, per *Bloomberg Businessweek*, an "unauthorized middlemen who had run afoul of the Federation in the past and paid thousands of dollars in fines." The contraband syrup ended up in a warehouse in New Brunswick whose proprietor regularly purchased syrup not authorized for release by the Federation—that business, as it is not in Quebec, isn't subject to the Federation's reach. The recipient was charged with intentionally receiving stolen property, but denied any knowledge as to the origins of the syrup.

BONUS FACT

Making maple syrup can get you in trouble in other ways. In February 2013, drug enforcement agents raided the Union County, Illinois, home of Laura Benson and her family. Their neighbors had called authorities, accusing the Bensons of running a meth lab out of their house. But police found no meth—only maple syrup. The family had a homemade syrup lab up and running. They took the raid in stride, giving some syrup to the police—not as evidence but for their breakfasts.

OIL BARON
HOW TO USE SALAD OIL TO
DEFRAUD YOUR CUSTOMERS

When we think of oil barons, we think of people who make a living and then some in the petroleum business. But in 1955, Tino De Angelis decided that another oil was worth his investment: vegetable oil. It made him a lot of money—and, eventually, also led him to prison.

In 1954, the United States enacted a law called the Agricultural Trade Development Assistance Act, which would lead to the creation of the Food for Peace program. The program provided an avenue for the sale of surplus goods to friendly nations, at that time typically European ones. De Angelis created a company called the Allied Crude Vegetable Oil Refining Corporation, which took advantage of the program by creating and exporting huge amounts of vegetable shortening and vegetable oil to allies in Europe, much of it substandard.

De Angelis's company took off and, over the next few years, became a major player in the vegetable oil market. In 1962, he made a successful attempt to corner the market, buying massive amounts of vegetable oil from other vendors. With his inventory now large enough to dictate the price of the oil, De Angelis had another idea: buy vegetable oil futures, which were still trading for cheap (but would soon be worth much, much more), cornering the market on the oil used in salad dressing. To finance this, De Angelis took out loans with his stock of vegetable oil as collateral.

However, to get the requisite amount of money loaned, De Angelis needed a lot more vegetable oil than Allied owned, even after the company bought the stores of other vendors. De Angelis turned to fraud (later dubbed the "salad oil scandal"), claiming to own much more vegetable oil than he did—in fact, the amount he stated he had was more than the Department of Agriculture believed was in the United States as a whole. Nevertheless, De Angelis invited his chief creditor, American Express, to inspect his warehouse and oil tanks (as they would have in the normal course of business anyway), and American Express dipped into the oil tanks, determined that there was, indeed, vegetable oil in them, and concluded that everything was on the up and up. Unbeknownst to AmEx, De Angelis had filled most of the tanks with water, but included enough oil that it, being less dense, would float to the top and mask the contents of the liquid lying below.

After a while, AmEx's inspectors were tipped off to the fraud, confirming it in a surprise inspection. Suddenly, the house of cards crumbled, setting off a catastrophic shockwave. The futures market for vegetable oil crashed, as did American Express's stock price—by a ridiculous 50 percent. De Angelis's company declared bankruptcy, and De Angelis himself served seven years in prison for his fraudulent dealings.

BONUS FACT

American Express got its start in Albany, New York, in 1850—well before the advent of credit cards (which developed in earnest in the 1920s and 1930s). In fact, it did not start out as a financial institution at all. Rather, AmEx's first business was in shipping—literally, "express mail." The company did not enter the financial services sector until 1882, when it branched out, slightly, into a money order business.

ONION RING
WHY YOU CAN'T TRADE ONION FUTURES IN THE USA

If you have seen the classic Eddie Murphy/Dan Aykroyd/Jamie Lee Curtis movie *Trading Places*—or, if you are simply knowledgeable about commodities trading—you probably know what "futures" and "shorting" are. If not, a "future" is a contract to buy a certain commodity at a preset date in the future at a price set today. The buyer of this contract hopes that the commodity's price will go up during the interim, whereas the contract's seller hopes it will go down. "Shorting" (or "short selling") happens when a seller of a stock or, in this case, of a futures contract, does not yet own what he or she is selling. Instead, the seller borrows the commodity futures from its owner, sells it, and then buys it back later. The short seller hopes that the price of the commodity will go down between when he or she borrows it and when he or she repurchases it, thereby making a pretty penny on the difference.

In the movie, Aykroyd and Murphy are trading futures of pork bellies and frozen concentrated orange juice. In fact, futures of almost all commodities can be purchased on public markets. Almost all, because in the United States at least, onion futures are prohibited from trade—thanks to Dwight Eisenhower, Gerald

Ford, and a pair of traders who gamed the system and walked away millionaires.

In 1955, onions made up 20 percent of the commodities traded at the Chicago Mercantile Exchange. Two traders, Sam Seigel and Vincent Kosuga, saw an opportunity. The pair began buying onions and onion futures in huge amounts, cornering the market. By that fall, they ended up with roughly 98 percent of all the onions in Chicago, totaling roughly 30 million pounds of the vegetable.

Soon after, Seigel and Kosuga started to short sell onion futures, effectively betting that the price of onions was about to drop precipitously. This was not a blind gamble, however. The pair began to sell their stockpiled onions, causing a glut of supply, and forcing the price of onions down—way down. In August 1955, a fifty-pound bag of onions in Chicago cost about $2.75. By March 1956 (when onion season ended), due to Seigel and Kosuga's market manipulation, the going rate in Chicago for the same amount of onions was a mere 10 cents. The pair walked away millionaires and left the onion market in shambles—worthless in Chicago and impossible to find everywhere else. The onion producers were going out of business, and they turned to Congress.

Gerald Ford, then a Congressman from Michigan, sponsored a bill outlawing the trade of onion futures—a very specific bill aimed at preventing this type of endeavor. The commodities trading lobby, of course, opposed the bill, threatening litigation if it were signed into law. President Eisenhower called their bluff, signing the Onion Futures Act in the summer of 1958. The Mercantile Exchange sued and lost. The trading of onion futures is banned in the United States to this day.

But the movie industry, at least, is better off for it. Because the Onions Future Act robbed the Mercantile Exchange of a robust market—and therefore, profit center—its leadership needed to expand the offerings in order to maintain a healthy business. The two most notable additions: pork bellies and frozen concentrated orange juice, the two key items traded in *Trading Places*.

BONUS FACT

In *Trading Places*, Aykroyd and Murphy's characters make their killing by engaging in insider trading—they are privy to an advance version of the orange crop report. One would think that, had they been caught, they would go to prison, but this is not the case. As of 2010, insider trading was not, generally speaking, illegal in commodities markets. In fact, that year, the head of the U.S. Commodity Futures Trading Commission testified in front of Congress arguing that this should be changed, and in his testimony, he cited the scheme pulled off in *Trading Places*.

LIFT OFF
WHEN CHICAGO RAISED ITS BUILDINGS

The city of Chicago was founded in 1833 on the coast of Lake Michigan and within the Mississippi River watershed. Its location—near rivers that lead south and adjacent to a conduit eastward—facilitated the city's rapid growth. Only 200 people were living in Chicago at its founding on August 12, 1833, but by 1840, well over 4,000 people lived there. By 1860, Chicago had 112,000 residents.

But growth comes with a price, especially in a city that is just five hundred feet or so (182 meters) above sea level. When it rained, the city flooded. Everywhere. Into the 1850s, Chicago did not have a working municipal sewage system. So water just collected and collected. Where water sits, disease brews, as Chicagoans quickly learned. Typhoid fever, dysentery, and cholera struck the city year after year. In 1854, a cholera outbreak killed as much as 6 percent of the city's population. Fixing the problem, though, presented another problem—how do you build sewers where the buildings already exist?

The solution: raise the buildings.

No, not raze. Raise, as in lift up. If the city could figure out a way to elevate four- and five-story (and larger!) buildings a few feet, they could install new foundations, allowing for the construction of a municipal sewage system. A few years later, they did exactly that. In January 1858, the first building—a four-story brick structure weighing 750 tons—was placed on 250 jackscrews and successfully lifted more than six feet above its original height without damaging it.

Over the next decade, much of central Chicago was similarly lifted so that the sewage system could be constructed. Most impressive, perhaps, was the lifting of a row of buildings 320 feet (nearly 100 meters) long on Lake Street—accomplished by roughly 600 men over the course of five days. In other cases, the city also had to raise the sidewalks, roads, and anything else installed too low for a sewer system to run underneath as well.

In general, the lifting was successful; there are few reports of damage. The city saw the lifting as an opportunity to do something else: It gentrified. Wooden-frame buildings, which were looked at as lesser, poorer structures than the brick-and-iron ones, were lifted—then removed, driven out of the city. As Wikipedia notes, the practice of putting these buildings "on rollers and moving them to the outskirts of town or to the suburbs was so common as to be considered nothing more than routine traffic."

BONUS FACT

If you're ever in Chicago, try the garlic and onions. The word "Chicago" comes from a Native American word *shikaakwa* (say it aloud), which over time became the term we know today. *Shikaakwa* means either wild garlic or wild onion, both of which were plentiful in the region before settlers of European descent arrived in the area.

SKYSCRAPER CAPER
THE SECRET PLAN TO FIX A
NEW YORK CITY SKYSCRAPER

Go to the corner of 53rd Street and Lexington Avenue in Manhattan, look up, and you'll see the Citigroup Center, a large white building—one of the ten tallest skyscrapers in the city—with its trademark angled roof, sloping at a 45-degree angle. At fifty-nine floors, the tower is home to well over a million square feet of office space, and its sloping top makes it a distinctive part of the New York City skyline. Construction on the building began in 1974 and was completed in 1977 at the total cost of just under $200 million. The Citigroup Center, like most other buildings, is designed to last for years to come.

Especially once the powers that be surreptitiously fixed the massive engineering mistake that would have otherwise doomed the skyscraper.

The Citigroup Center is, architecturally, different than most buildings. Whereas the typical building has structural support columns at each of the four corners, the Citigroup Center's columns are in the center of each of the four sides, allowing the building to cantilever over a neighboring church. Doing so required a special type of bracket, which the building's structural engineer, William

LeMessurier, designed for this specific purpose. As designed, the building could sustain a direct, straight-on hit from hurricane-level winds.

Unfortunately, the construction company never tested to see how the building would fare against winds that hit the building at a 45-degree angle, which would cause the winds to hit two of the four outer walls simultaneously. After this concern was brought to LeMessurier's attention—and well after the building was finished—he tested the theory in a wind tunnel and determined that these "quartering winds" would cause significantly more load than anticipated. But because the building, as drawn up, was padded with a significant level of additional safety measures, this theoretical problem had few if any practical ramifications.

Until, that is, someone mentioned to LeMessurier about a cost savings the builders had found. Instead of welding his special brackets onto the structural columns, the builders bolted them on. Welded brackets are less likely to fall prey to heavy winds. When faced with the same hurricane-level force, bolts have the potential to shear. And no one tested to see if the bolts could handle hurricane-level quartering winds. In theory? They couldn't.

That June, LeMessurier determined that the type of winds capable of causing structural damage to the building hit Manhattan every fifteen to twenty years. Having a fifty-nine-story building in the middle of Manhattan that was at risk for such damage was, to say the least, a very big problem. Hurricane season was only a few months away. With a 5–10 percent chance of a building-threatening storm coming that fall, fixing the problem became a priority. But admitting to it was an embarrassment. In addition, telling the public would likely cause a panic among neighbors and office workers alike. So LeMessurier and Citicorp (as it was then known) agreed to do the repairs after-hours, and not tell anyone.

It took three months, but the secret workmen successfully welded steel plates over the bolted-on brackets. No one found out about the fix-up job for nearly two decades; *The New Yorker* broke the story in 1995. And no one was hurt by the faulty building.

BONUS FACT

The angled roof of the Citigroup Center was not, originally, intended for simple aesthetics, but rather to provide a home for solar panels. No solar panels are there, though, because the roof is positioned in such a way that it never receives adequate sunlight for solar panels to provide a worthwhile amount of power.

TO INFINITY AND BEYOND
THE RACE TO BUILD THE
TALLEST BUILDING IN THE WORLD

On New Year's Day, 1930, the world's tallest building was Manhattan's Woolworth Building, at a height of 792 feet. As advancements in architecture emerged, so did the desire to top the heights reached by the Woolworth Building. In late 1928, two competing teams broke ground with plans for buildings that, if completed as designed, would easily surpass Woolworth's mark. The race was on.

And trickery was on the agenda.

Originally, the Chrysler Building wasn't supposed to be the Chrysler Building. The architect, a man named William Van Alen, had designed some plans for a contractor named William H. Reynolds, who was looking to build an office building. At 807 feet tall, Van Alen's proposed building would be taller than the Woolworth Building. But Reynolds thought the plan would cost too much and might not be possible. He sold the plans to Walter Chrysler, the founder of the Chrysler Corporation. Chrysler envisioned the creation of a future headquarters for his car company—a jewel among skyscrapers known throughout the world. An 800-something-foot building sounded like a great start, but both Chrysler and Van Alen wanted to push to the limits. Van Alen went back to the drawing board (literally). His revised plan put the building at 925 feet.

Around the same time, H. Craig Severance, also an architect, began a rival project at 40 Wall Street (which the building is often called today), known then as the Bank of Manhattan Trust Building. This building was, originally, designed to be 840 feet. But upon learning that the Chrysler Building would soar eight-five feet higher than their construction, Severance and his team revised their plans, adding three extra stories. The completed Bank of Manhattan Trust Building, upon its opening in April of 1930, was 927 feet, then the tallest building in the world. The Chrysler Building, which wouldn't open for another month, was not going to pass it, given everything that the Bank of Manhattan Trust team knew.

But they didn't know everything. Chrysler and Van Alen had secretly constructed a 125-foot-tall spire, made for the top of the building, within the building itself. Almost no one outside the project knew about it, and the secrecy involved kept Severance and company from adjusting their plans. When the Chrysler Building installed the spire in October of 1929, construction on the Bank of Manhattan Trust Building was too far along to revise the plans again.

The Chrysler Building opened on May 27, 1930 at a height of 1,048 feet—not only taking the title of "tallest building in the world" from its downtown rival, but also surpassing the Eiffel Tower as the tallest man-made structure on the planet at the time. Severance took exception to their claim, however, arguing that the spire was nothing more than decorative; his building's highest accessible floor was 100 feet higher than Chrysler's.

That nuance, while still in debate when determining what constitutes the tallest building in the world today, was quickly rendered moot. On April 30, 1931, the Empire State Building—1,224 feet to the top floor, 1,250 feet to the roof, and 1,454 feet to the tip of the antenna spire—topped both buildings, by any measure.

BONUS FACT

The Empire State Building set a new height record, but its architects weren't above some chicanery themselves. The top of the building was originally designed, at least superficially, to be a landing moor for dirigibles (that is, Zeppelins), giving passengers a way to enter midtown Manhattan in style. According to *The New York Times*, the dirigible moor was nothing more than an excuse to make the building an extra 200 feet taller in order to surpass the height record set by the Chrysler Building. No airships ever docked at the Empire State Building, as conditions were quickly deemed unsafe for such activities.
